THE MUSEUM DOSE

12 EXPERIMENTS IN PHARMACOLOGICALLY MEDIATED AESTHETICS

Daniel Tumbleweed

Curated by J.P. Harpignies

ISBN: 0692446443
ISBN-13: 978-0-692-44644-7

For all those who guided me safely in—

Exhibits

Curator's Preface

I feel quite confident in asserting that you, dear reader, have never read a book like this one. It is in a category all its own. When I first saw an early version of what became the first piece in this collection, I immediately felt that this young man possessed a distinctive, offbeat, but deeply refined voice. His forays into artistic appreciation filtered through a truly unusual lens were unlike anything I had run across. Some aspects of his ruminations will be familiar to anyone who has been exposed to the discourse of the contemporary subterranean countercultural intelligentsia, but in my view his sensitivity reflects the most interesting, highest octaves of that milieu, so I encouraged him to produce more pieces and suggested that perhaps we could put them out as a collection if he generated a sufficient quantity of work.

I have never consumed any of the substances the author ingests in these experiments. My wild countercultural days are, sadly perhaps, due to my antiquity, in the distant past, and back in the 1960s and 70s, none of these particular molecules had yet been fashioned, and even then I tended to be more interested in visionary plants than in synthetic drugs. Unlike some of the potential readership of this tome, at this stage of my life it is not the drugs described herein that are of particular interest to me, it is the sensibility of the writer as he intentionally puts himself in a vulnerable emotional state to deepen his aesthetic experiences and allow art works to challenge him to his core. It is that raw courage and emotional honesty, as well as his rather unfashionable complete lack of irony or posturing that I find most affecting.

This is on one hand a contemporary account of self-discovery, a search for meaning and a place in the world of a young man on the cusp of true adulthood in the context of the crushing alienation and the infinite possibilities of the modern megalopolis. It is also a quintessential New York book, a beautifully heartfelt paean to the city I have lived in my entire life. He viscerally captures the city's pulse and its infinite layers, and the hopes, anxieties, joys, terrors and surprises one can't help but find in its streets, especially if one's eyes and heart are more open than usual (not always recommended).

To be clear: My involvement in this project does not imply that I in any way advocate that others run out and emulate this approach to art immersion. Understandably perhaps, some artists and writers throughout the centuries, from Coleridge and Rimbaud to Huxley, Ginsberg, Burroughs, to Kesey and Pynchon, et al, have been tempted to alter perceptions with whatever radical means were at hand. Seeing the world in new ways is after all the artist's mandate, and it's not surprising that the most unconstrained among them will seek to use any means necessary to that end. This has produced some interesting results as well as quite a few dead-ends and ruined lives. Many artists' stories of wild experimentation wind up being cautionary tales, but not all do.

In this instance, I can't be sure, but I sense in this young man a deep abiding sanity and healthy psychic core, so I suspect this stage in his life will wind up being a productive phase of youthful experimentation, reminiscent of the illustrious but relatively short lived mid-19th Century Parisian circle of hashish users that included Baudelaire, Gautier,

Dumas, de Nerval, Hugo, Balzac, and Delacroix, all of whom were briefly very interested in the aesthetic lenses provided by altered states. I'm not of course comparing our budding writer to that immortal, but Baudelaire also devoted much of his work to art criticism and described his mental states as he wandered the streets of Paris at night. In any case, it would be a terrible shame if the controversial nature of the method he has used in these experiments caused some otherwise refined readers to eschew this tome, because this promising, open-hearted, deeply intelligent, sensitive young writer's first work is filled with insights, humor, beauty, and flashes of luminous brilliance.

J.P. Harpignies, Brooklyn, NY, May 2015

A day at the Stanford museum. Things were visually rich, yet I felt that I was reasonably inconspicuous. The Rodin sculptures were very personal and not terribly subtle. I saw Escher things in the ceiling design, when I decided to sit in a foyer somewhere and simply pretend to rest. Walking back, the displays seen in the bark of the eucalyptus trees, and the torment and fear (of others? of themselves?) in the faces of those who were walking towards us, were as dramatic as anything I had seen in the art galleries. Our appetites were enormous, and we went to a smorgasbord that evening. A rich experience in every possible way.

Dr. Alexander Shulgin
"2C-B"
Phenethylamines I Have Known and Loved

Clavier-Übung III
Alice Tully Hall
25mg 4-AcO-DMT

In the plaza outside Lincoln Center, I paused by the fountain and withdrew one small gel capsule from my jeans pocket. The pill, a gift from an amateur pharmacologist, contained 25 milligrams of 4-acetoxy-dimethyltryptamine. I held it up against the amber halo of a streetlamp before eating it, noting that the powder barely occupied one eighth of the capsule. A strong dose, I had been told.

Tonight, I would attend the christening of the newly reinstalled concert organ at Alice Tully Hall. Four thousand one hundred and ninety-two pipes of meticulous Swiss construction, it had been dismantled, refurbished, and fine-tuned over the last five years. The performance was of a work by J.S. Bach that I had never heard before: Clavier-Übung III, considered one of the composer's most complex collections of organ compositions.

I walked a few languorous laps around the plaza to shake off the jitters, then made my way into the concert hall. The building leaned askew. I navigated through a flurry of well-heeled strangers, peering into their distorted faces. The inevitable thought crept up as they stared back—do they know? Walking became an ordeal, the routine mechanics now requiring considerable attention. I weaved along an endless elastic corridor that mercifully yielded at long last to a bustling wooden auditorium. An usher greeted me, handed me a playbill and showed me to my row.

Approaching my seat, I beamed a smile at my neighbor for the evening. Plump and middle-aged, she was draped in feathers, gems, and sequins from head to toe. She looked at me, then at the empty seat beside her, and bristled. When I sat down, she shifted her weight to the armrest further from me and buried her face in her program. Her eyebrows arched and her features pulled to the bulb of her nose as she made every effort to focus on the playbill and keep me out of her visual periphery.

My attention swung to the stage. Built into the heart of it stood the organ, an archangel of wood and silver with wings of metal cylinders spread wide. The vast array of pipes stood open-mouthed, begging to sing. They ranged in size from miniscule to colossal. They waited patiently for the one who would breathe air into their lungs.

Framing the stage, the wood paneled walls of the auditorium radiated warmth. Stark lines of light emerged from points along their lengths and carved the room into geometric shapes that seemed to be drawn to and coalesced around the many open mouths of the organ. Whenever the din of the room bubbled louder, this field of vectors quivered, as if all of our voices were strings upon a harp. Layers of conversation slipped across my eardrums and I surrendered to the bedlam of sound waves, not trying to parse or make sense of all the beautiful noise.

My neighbor sighed loudly and clicked her tongue. My fingers gripped the armrest on either side of me. My nerves were alight. I stilled my fidgeting and busied myself by watching the human traffic buzzing among the rows. The men seemed stern, exuding ownership. The women wore scarves and outsized rings, some stylish, some just ostentatious. Dressed to the nines, one and all. I sat in my faded jeans and white hooded sweatshirt, my curly shock of hair unkempt, and felt much the outlier. I hadn't shaved in months.

My neighbor's friends arrived, returning from the bar with drinks, and whispered amongst themselves. The drug hit me in waves now and I yawned with the full force of my being. The woman glanced at me over her shoulder, the entire coterie following her gaze with eyebrows arched.

They shook their heads as one and she, my neighbor, pulled a pair of horn-rimmed glasses from a leather case. Our eyes met once more and her body ruffled. Her plumpness drew itself into pointed corners. She pushed her glasses up her nose, pushed her nose up her face, and sank it in her program once more.

Black fuzz bled around the perimeter of her being, an inverse lightning that crackled into the space all around me. The once-harmonious din of the crowd grew fractured and dissonant. The room lurched. I closed my eyes and deepened my breathing, trying to visualize the synthetic tryptamine tickling my synapses. I filtered out the noise and the worry, grounding myself in the moment. When I opened my eyes again, an intricate latticework spiraled out from my chest. The organ, my uptight neighbor, the tryptamine, and soon, Bach. I was at the center of a mandala.

Just then the room dimmed, the murmur of the crowd hushed to a whisper. White beams of light illuminated the organ from below. The wings of the stage folded open and the virtuoso organist appeared, dressed like a Lutheran schoolboy in pleated khakis and a simple white dress shirt. He ascended the staircase to take his throne before the keys and pedals of the archangel. In a flurry of activity, the audience rushed to clear their throats and noses. No longer pulsing at the periphery of my consciousness, the drug now came on in earnest, triggered by the auditorium's transformation.

The organist hiked his cuffs up his wrists and pressed his weight into the keys.

The curtains on creation blew aside. A cavalry of pipes called to the sky, trumpeting my arrival to the vaulted clouds above, summoning a staircase that bloomed at my feet and rose into the depths of the firmament. There were no builders, just the steps and balustrade willing themselves into being and beckoning me forward. I climbed into the infinite, pausing in sonic plateaus that stretched just long enough for me to catch my breath and steel my nerves for the next ascent. Shafts of light crashed down through stained glass fog. I climbed, approaching but never nearing the foot of some distant and unknowable throne.

The organ hummed and moaned and sighed in overlapping tones that swelled to fill the space between all things. A rush of air sighed past my lips to join the swirling notes, carrying me with it. The auditorium swam with stories, encoded in sound, summoned from the minds of those in the audience and carried away on notes written long ago. I followed these tales, riding currents of thought and noise, feeling avian and meandering with soft purpose just above the surface of a shimmering cloud cover.

The agony of being alive had never been so bearable. Poppies bloomed, cities fell, stars collapsed into themselves. The minutiae of existence built to a crescendo of cosmic significance. I rose out from the crown of my skull and hovered over the rows ahead to mount the stage and sit beside the organist. Here was Bach himself, christening the organ at St. Boniface centuries ago, his fingers dancing over the keys in staccato rushes. He was our lifeline, the bridge between the known and the Mystery. Nature crested in him, flowing through the organ, mapped in patterns writ in our blood. Clusters of fibrous nerves and layers of tissue and bone beneath my skin attuned themselves to that same harmony. My body responded to the call of the organ. Pared down to nothingness, I carved myself in its image.

Centering myself in breath, I pulled back a thousand pieces of myself from the emotion condensing in the room. It was all in my quivering hands, all my own. The yawning divide between myself and the Creator disappeared. There was no divide, there was only the power of holding this space inside this body. I looked to the stage. The organist shook his head, nodding to the organ. The archangel opened its jaws and called out to Bach. Bach bowed low, lifting a hand to the sky. The sky in turn descended to become me.

Clavier-Übung III closed with a fugue. Two voices joined in counterpoint and hand in hand began the final ascent up the cliffs of the holy mountain. The procession swelled inside me. All of the world's chaos was merely order on a level I could only fleetingly perceive, all entwined in an alchemical helix, reaching tirelessly for the beyond. The organist wended his way through the labyrinth of the fugue, taking us all on a grand chase. The Omega point approached, pulling audience and organ forward in time. The final chords sounded out, infusing me with ultimate wonder and infinite enthusiasm for the joy of being human. A newborn star bloomed at the heart of the stage. I felt the seat beneath me quivering, pulled towards that gravity well. The last tone died to silence.

Rapturous applause.

After the curtain calls, I reached down beneath my seat to gather up my jacket. My neighbor looked up at me over her shoulder, her eyes widening just as they had at our first encounter. Then she turned away with a smirk, leaning in close to her associates. I took a step towards her and leaned down, touching her shoulder gently.

"Wasn't that just fantastic?" I said, flashing a broad and sincere smile.

In the lobby, waiters hustled by with trays of champagne flutes. Women wrapped themselves in heavy furs. People tilted their heads back and laughed. Words were everywhere, babbling brooks of language I could see flowing from mouth to ear. I could barely form a thought. Through the glass enclosure I could see a deluge drenching the city.

I stepped outside, ducking under an overhang. The cacophony of voices disappeared behind me, replaced by the rhythm of falling water and the splash of passing taxis. I leaned against the glass façade of the building.

I couldn't imagine listening to music ever again. The rush of raindrops breaking open against concrete sounded perfect. I raised my arms over my head, stretching them to the ends of their sockets and spreading my fingers wide, pushing out to the very edges of myself.

I looked out at the sheets of water falling on Broadway. The downpour was daunting. I caught a taxi and settled into the back seat. Alice Tully Hall pulled away behind me as the cab joined a fleet of yellow metal headed downtown. I looked out the window at the passing cityscape. Lakes formed at corners, cabs jockeyed for position, and pedestrians hustled to stay dry out on the sidewalks. The ride home was slow, but I was in no rush at all.

Brian Eno's 77 Million Paintings
Café Rouge
18 mg 2c-t-2

Buried deep in midtown, the door to "77 Million Paintings" was unassuming if not quite dingy. The glass doors were tinted black with two small stickers affixed below eye level advertising the exhibit. A bored security guard sat on a metal folding chair just inside, yawning as he asked me to silence my cell phone. Walking past him through the entrance, I found myself in an antechamber draped in pitch darkness. The initial effect, especially coming in out of the busy Manhattan daylight, was disconcerting.

I followed a distant echoing sound and passed through a curtain into the cavernous exhibit space. This room had once been the Café Rouge, a restaurant within the New Yorker Pennsylvania Hotel. Once home to glitzy, jazz-era parties, it was now transformed (and had been for the past five weeks) into an ambient meditative space designed by musician, artist, and nearly mythic contemporary Renaissance man Brian Eno.

I had seen Eno speak earlier in the week at Cooper Union's Great Hall. I was well versed in Eno the musician, both his solo rock and ambient works as well as his producer credits on albums by such luminaries as Talking Heads, David Bowie, U2, etc.. The lecture had walked the audience from Eno's birth through the course of a lifetime of work, leading to his current experiments in visual art and ambient experiences, known as 77 Million Paintings.

The installation transforms each time Eno brings it to a new home. It has even been projected across the fractal conch surface of the iconic Sydney Opera House, but for now it was in this much more inconspicuous locale, tucked away where one might least expect it to be found.

The 2c-t-2 was slow in coming on, but looking back now I realize that my initial sense of displacement in the antechamber to 77 Million Paintings was heightened by the first tentative rushes of this new (to me) psycholytic compound. I followed some echoing tones into the main room. They sounded rung through tunnels far away, perhaps piped in from a Tibetan monastery halfway across the world.

Two couches and two lounge seats, dark red, sat far back from the central visual element of the exhibit. I made out three or four silhouetted heads in the penumbra. I navigated to an empty seat on a couch and settled in. The muggy summer day outside still clung to my clothes and my clothes to my skin. I looked upon the centerpiece, the slowly transforming digital painting set into the far wall, and breathed.

At first, I felt the same nagging worry I feel whenever I sit to meditate—that I will never be able to calm myself enough to still the torrential rush of my inner chatter. And the onset of a new drug invariably produces anxiety—after all, one can never know just from research and reading what to expect, how the wave will flow once it has broken. I watched the "painting."

It was made of pieces, and the pieces failed to impress. The whole painting had a shape similar to a swastika, tilted on its axis with its angles shifted around. An off-kilter cross sat in the middle, glowing a solid purple. Around it, in a radial design fitting into its ninety-degree angles, was a set of four rectangles. Another set of four branched out from there, and a final set of four from there. The shape reminded me of those Japanese *shuriken* throwing weapons made famous by trashy movies about ninjas, or a flower or star.

Each of the rectangles in each set of four displayed the same image, but each set of rectangles showed something entirely different. These images, I knew, were being pulled from a vast library of even smaller components, and fed into the digital painting by randomized algorithms that created 77 million—or more—possibilities. The solid purple cross at this moment was fringed by imagery in the rectangles that were reminiscent of amoebae, pebbles, plant life, trellises. The subway and the outside still clung to me, clung to my breathing, and my thoughts were drifting out to mundane things far away—my laundry, an email I had just sent.

But then the sound in the room caught my attention. Speakers were mounted everywhere—up, down, left, right, and the sounds emanating from them evoked space and movement: a gong slowly dwindling away, threatening to fall into silence, replaced by a soft digital squiggle, yawning, like sound breaking apart across vast expanses between circuitry. The polygonal shapes on the wall started melding with the sounds moving back and forth.

And then everything shifted. The thing on the wall out beyond a vast expanse of pitch-black floor was not the thing I had been looking at a moment before. The cross at the center was mauve now, and graffiti stick figures, origami flowers, microscopic zoom-ins of bacteria, were spiraling out from it.

I felt wide, stretched. This was a smooth drug, without an agenda or a push. The wave had broken, but the sea was calm. I watched pieces of the painting, scrutinizing them, focusing in on the smallest elements, waiting for them to change. I heard the sound of a heavy object hurtling through space, past my ear, behind me. The blues and piercing yellows and greens were gone and now I saw cold colors, circuitry layered over cartoon triangles, fragments of some unrecognized language.

When I put my attention on the center, the anatomical snapshots of mythical creatures and the Caribbean stick figures and the ultraviolet photostats surrounding it blended into perfect focus. The solid center slowly faded from green to red to brown to blue, and I followed it.

A very faint human voice came calling out of the sonic aether in which I was swimming. It felt like an ancient soul reincarnated in the depths of vast electronic machinery, trying to sing out longingly to its lost gods, but with its voice broken into strange fragments drifting across the room. The heavy object I had heard earlier seemed to whirl through space again, whoosh, whoosh, whoosh, in a slow gyroscopic trajectory.

I broke my eyes from the center. They once again wandered the rectangular fields of texture and pattern—tangled messes of tentacles and vectors, solid beams of light, paper-mâché clouds, stencils of sinking ships. Turkish rugs danced in my vision. My gaze moved clockwise around the resplendent shuriken, and by the time it completed a full circuit the whole palette had changed, and I couldn't remember what it had been. Everything that had passed before me was gone, and I couldn't remember…

This drove home that though I didn't feel as though I were dying, it was impossible to ignore the fact that one day I would. The sounds circling the room like spirits were warm, but they offered little comfort. Everything in the room was fading, every moment falling through to the next. What was this thing in front of me? Sometimes I lost interest in it, but then I would blink and it suddenly controlled me completely, and I was speechless, awestruck.

I focused on the center once again, and it faded from color into darkness. The twelve rectangles of the tilted star seemed on the verge of scattering off into space, but the invisible center was a sure thing. It was there; it could be counted on. I saw myself in it. The ancient soul's cry reached out again, but I felt now that perhaps it wasn't mourning the dead, but the living. Me.

People were coming and going. Some walked close to the construct on the wall, but most kept their distance, reverent. Eventually, though, a clicking noise began. And for all the digital nature of this piece, the mechanical sound of someone's telephoto lens seemed invasive, harsh. The photographer moved around the room, snapping shots of the thing, not understanding that he was capturing nothing. The moments between his shutter snapping were the sum of it, and he couldn't grasp that.

I walked out on to the street to find that the city was wet. There had been a massive thunderstorm; buildings were dripping down into the black asphalt of the streets, water running into dirty gutters. I stood frozen, unsure how to re-enter the stream. I checked the time and blinked upon discovering that while I had sat there, searching for stillness, five hours had passed.

Pantha du Prince and The Bell Laboratory
West Park Presbyterian Church
12mg 2c-i

At the West Park Presbyterian Church on New York's Upper West Side, the German house DJ Pantha du Prince was set to perform the New York debut of his new opus, a composition written for electronics and bells called Elements of Light, created with a collective of percussionists known as the Bell Laboratory.

The arrangement is meant to explore, through five tracks of sound, the various elements of light: Wave, Particle, Photon, Spectral Split, Quantum.

I started feeling tightness in my ribs: with each breath, I felt my body constricting while my head expanded, that uncomfortable vasoconstrictive quality that accompanies many phenethylamine experiences.

The city was damp, and puddles of recent rain seemed to tilt ever so slightly away from me as the sidewalk stretched a little longer with each step I took. Behind an ugly skirt of low scaffolding, West Park Presbyterian Church's domed bell-tower rose above the corner of 86th St. and Amsterdam Ave, its ruddy sandstone kissed a deeper red by the sun's setting rays.

Once I climbed the church steps, it took my eyes a moment to adjust to the dim light of the interior. I walked through the rows of attendees and searched out an empty seat, settling into the rigid demands of the church pews, physically uncomfortable enough but also always awkward for this secular Jew. It was a small church with few seats but tall, cavernous ceilings. I starting feeling myself swelling up into the empty space above the pews, towards the rafters, the belfry, the stained glass windows.

A playground, or a laboratory, had been erected on the floor of the church around and upon its pulpit. Bells. Hundreds of them, different shapes and sizes, attached to various apparatuses. A white curtain, affixed at every foot or so to a wire running above it, loomed above the stage like a Greek chorus, brushing at the bottom edge of a radiant stained glass window portraying Matthew 17:14, in which Jesus heals an epileptic boy. On either side of this luminescent glass, the copper mouths of the church organ filled two windows to bursting, the organ itself hidden behind the curtain.

I leafed idly through a hymnal found in the back of the pew ahead of mine, tracing my fingers over the unfamiliar phrases, watching curlicues of shadow skim out from around my fingertips. The room was dark but I felt my eyes dilating, pulsing, grabbing light from the strangest places. My calves and hamstrings felt tight, my torso uncomfortable, as if perhaps my body had shrunk down to one size too small, pressuring my organs to find new ways of leaning up against one another. My head was immense, becoming the architecture all around me, and felt on the verge of a headache that mercifully never came.

Like the sun announcing its arrival with the lightening of the sky over a distant horizon, the concert began at the fringes of the church. No lighting was dimmed, no announcement was made. The din of conversation melted to a rapt silence as awarenesses were drawn to the corners of the pulpit, out of which walked six men in coveralls one would expect to be seen worn by the workers in a foundry. They walked slowly, one by one, each man with a hand-bell in each hand. These they flicked against the space in front of them, summoning tones from the still air of the church.

Standing in front of all the bells and toys spread out along the pulpit and the floor around it, the six "scientists" stared into a nothing-space out in front of them, whipping their bells with a strength that belied the soft sounds evinced from them. Each tingle and chime drifted out, willing all to silence. I felt the ringing of the metal passing through me, dying slowly, waning and decaying, only to find myself washed over by the sound of another tone, and another, and another—Wave.

Then a conversation began to blossom, one spoken in the sine waves of sound, the various vibrations washing over each other and blending together. At first no two tones were rung at the same time, but soon the bells rang in chords, harmonizing. My bones, still held taut by anxious muscles, quivered like tuning forks under the gentle pressure of the glowing tones that reverberated around me. The six gentlemen, their overalls covering white work-suits, seemed to be plucking invisible strings suspended in the space all around them.

The men dispersed, each walking to a separate workstation. One, the oldest-looking, with a grizzled beard, sat down to a drum kit rigged with shakers, timpanis, log drums, and rack bells. Four more went to separate stations equipped with a panoply of percussive metal instruments while Pantha du Prince ascended the pulpit and awoke his laptop computer, slipping headphones into his ears.

The bell workers slowly built a rhythm. Tinkles and chimes gave way to clangs and rings, and the ambling sonic conversation gave way to a passage through a tunnel of rhythmic banging. Slippery noodles of electronica wormed their way along the passageway carved out by the bells, swiping and gurgling and then finally birthing a deep bass beat that thrummed deep into the floor of the church and seemed to shake its foundations. The deep, earthy counterpoint summoned all the bells towards it, dragging a weighty gravitational force through the soundscape—Particle.

The gentle bell-song of angels, now seduced by a giant writhing digital snake, mutated into a high-hat laden dance beat. Many sat still like good churchgoing folk, but I joined a scattering of others in the pews unable to sit still who weaved side to side in their seats. Far to stage right, one of the bell-men stood in a box-like structure, a carillon of fifty different bells. He held two mallets in each hand, turning and striking surfaces all around and above and below him precisely and fluidly.

Across the room, another member of the collective beat out harmonic tones on a massive xylophone the size of a grand piano, then turned to drag mallets across a rack of tubular bells All the percussionists, though now facing in every different direction, were still engaged in a vibrant conversation, only now they flew through space with this new and unfamiliar electronic creature, like plankton swimming alongside the massive form of a sperm whale, shaping their communal self along its mass.

Above it all, Pantha du Prince danced among his digital gadgets, his knobs and sliders and monomes. By far the youngest of the performers, he came across as an upstart entrant into God's kingdom, enticing the old guard of angels to come down to Earth and play a new kind of game rooted deep in the ground, far from their habitual clouds. As the song built, the bell sounds fractured from soft to hard, clanging, banging, jingling and jangling. The churchtower's own bell loomed over the heads of all, the giant steel elephant in the room.

The mountain range of curtains, the Greek chorus lofted behind the bell laboratory, shook with the thunderhead of bass notes that crashed again and again into the concrete floor of the building. A blink of my eyes brought scattershot kaleidoscopic images, which persisted when my eyes reopened. Mounted strobe lights flashed behind the organ pipes, and the afterimages shattered out across my vision.

Just before it all built to a crescendo, it broke back down, settling, melting off organically into nothing but the physical sound of wood striking metal. The bass died away.

Like monks in a slow procession, each of the Bell Lab's mad scientists broke away from his station, picking up a set of choir-chimes and walking back down towards the front and center of the stage, producing a tone, then a higher tone, and another, like climbing three steps of a ladder, over and over again. The six engaged again in conversation, only with higher, more potent tones, their new tools creating a chime that calmed my thoughts, breath, and beating heart—Photon.

I rode my breath to a more serene place, listening to the way each swelling tone built on the one that came before it, so that a still lake spreading all around us was bisected and broken up by gentle ripples bending into one another, sending out soft waves of motion in all directions. The building was stilled, like an anxious beast being coaxed to equanimity. The broken bits of my thoughts bled back into me and knit into a pattern I could understand.

But the choir of bell-ringers dispersed again, breaking off to their stations. I took a deep breath in anticipation of what I knew was coming, the most intense and longest portion of the composition—Spectral Split.

This time, it was the bells that guided the bass, luring it like a snake from a basket. It wove into the air, the pews, my feet, my bones. Whereas the bass of Particle had slammed down like a fist, here it felt as if it slipped down into the Earth and up again, buffeting me, lifting me, picking me up. The tinkle of all the bells around it had the joyous feeling of sun and sky.

A river of synthetic melody tumbled through the gentle hurricane of sound whipping all around me and through tears welling in my eyes I saw the meager light of the church refracted, magnified, broken apart. I watched it enter me like a prism and break into myriad component pieces, all the wavelengths and particles that make up a single stream of luminescence.

The baptism of percussion and light built in relentless crescendos that swallowed one another. Tubular bells, vibraphones, marimbas, gongs, drums, bass, my flesh, my past, my guilts, my loves—a flurry of all that I ever was and ever would be. I felt myself both here and not here at all, the transience of everything and the insistence of the now all rushing upwards in waves of sound from the soles of my feet to the crown of my head, breaking open to the sky. I watched the light inside me burst apart and knew that it was all right, that everything breaks, everything splits, but that it washes out in waves and when those waves dissipate, drifting into the ether, more waves will follow in their tracks.

Bass and synthetic rushes were the first to die away, vanishing beyond the fragmenting clangor of the bells and gongs and triangles and harps, all of which fell into a dissonant drone that clung to the walls of the church like moss. Like Catholic priests swinging censers, each of the six men picked up their hand bells and walked, breaking apart like molecules of ink in water, drifting among the pews. They stared straight ahead of themselves, making eye contact with no one, still touching the invisible, and rang the bells gently at us, the softest tones, the final blessings.

As one of them passed me by, I closed my eyes and felt the chime of his bell touch me right upon the forehead. Mellifluous waves of light rippled down through my skeleton and rose back up, clearing out the cobwebs in my belfry. I became a singing bowl, resounding that one glowing chime. The bells tinkled through the crowd, passing down each and every aisle and to the back of the church and then returning to the foot of the pulpit, where they stood in front of their laboratory and the final chimes folded themselves away into nothingness.

Outside, Amsterdam Avenue was insistently bright, and I quickly swung up to 87th Street and turned to slowly walk along its shadowed length. The night was quiet, and I watched the light play along the sidewalk, the facades of buildings and the layers of leaves sprouting from the late spring trees, flooding into any space it could reach. I had always thought of light as the exception and shadow the rule, but now I was not so sure.

At the threshold to Central Park I stood and stared down the length of the walkway drifting into the thick of the park. Farther south down Central Park West, light rushed in a river towards the acrid glow of Columbus Circle's billboards, fluorescent lights in cages beneath scaffolding, warmly lit windows, headlights and lampposts. I walked into the park, where the game between light and dark was playing by much older rules…

The Transfinite
Park Avenue Armory
12mg 4-HO-MPT, sleeplessness

I should have been sober. I'd taken twelve milligrams of 4-HO-MPT around 1 AM the previous night, and it was now nearing noon, but sleep had been elusive, and even as my fellow revelers had sunk into sleep on floors, couches, and beds, perhaps exhausted by other more physically demanding substances, I felt far from any sort of torpor. I stood out on the balcony of the DUMBO high-rise, watching the sun slog its way upwards through what seemed a particularly polluted summer morning in New York City.

The timeline for 4-HO-MPT should theoretically have seen me back at baseline hours before, but in my experience you're never really all the way back down until you sleep. I still felt tremors fluttering through my perceptions. If I unfocused my eyes and allowed my gaze to loosen, the distant lurid sunrise seemed to paradoxically reveal sharp, geometric outlines, a gridwork of light in the sky. At that moment I was almost thankful for the smog I had been breathing during my three decades in this effulgent, dirty city. The oranges and pinks it sometimes elicited at sunrise and sunset were magnificent, and through all the strata of car exhaust and air conditioner output, this morning sun's ascent rang triumphant.

I tiptoed through the sleeping, splayed bodies on the living room floor and made my way quietly outside. The world was stirring in the way it only does on Sunday mornings. The air was soup. My movements felt nearly unconscious, as if I had programmed my destination, the Park Avenue Armory, into my bones and muscles, and now they would carry me and all I had to do was let my mind float along. I walked against traffic down Flatbush Avenue, the harsh heat and glare of cars stabbing at my serenity but somehow deflected by a dizzied shield I had erected around myself.

As the space around me changed, so did my experience of the drug. It seemed to be clinging to my receptor sites like a mountain climber hugging a rock face, losing purchase only to grab another foothold. Ebbs and flows. Every step down the subway stairs seemed to recede as I lowered my foot towards it, and I had the sinking feeling the mouth of the cave would close behind me. The train came with merciful haste, but my relief at the air-conditioned respite it offered was overshadowed by the demands of being in public.

Feelings of heightened empathy left me staring at the floor, lest my unabashed curiosity tempt me into the taboo behavior of looking deeply into the eyes of every other straphanger and soaking up their pains and hurts. The subway is never an easy place to trip. People cloak themselves in a privacy that makes their dissatisfactions utterly transparent. It's a place in which people feel free to undergo a very solitary catharsis, but don't want to be bothered to know you might care.

I finally left the underground up into another world. The Upper East Side has its own Sunday morning rituals. Like the architecture and the fashion of the neighborhood, it all drips with money. Unshowered, I floated up the wide boulevard of Park Avenue, sweat pouring off me to mix into the general summer city broth, an urban bouillabaisse, though far less fragrant and tasty than that dish.

I'd never been to see an exhibition at the Park Avenue Armory before, and I didn't know what to expect of Ryoji Ikeda's "Transfinite." All I knew was that this Sunday was the end of its run, and a flyer I'd seen had aroused my curiosity. I ambled along the ticket line and then walked to the entrance of the Wade Thompson Drill Hall, approaching a pitch-black doorway from which vaguely ominous electronic noises were emerging.

The pitch darkness I had perceived was actually a heavy curtain, and I pushed it aside to step through.

The Wade Thompson Drill Hall is humongous, like an airplane hangar. In a city of shoebox apartments, to walk into such an expansive space is in itself transformative. The entire structure was draped in black, creating a cocoon-like feeling. I stood at the entrance to the womb, taking in the scene.

The initial impression was of walking into a church, albeit one housed on a distant platform orbiting a dying star, a church of and for techno-pilgrims, with ships launching from far flung galaxies to bow down before the intelligence at the core of the interstellar motherboard.

A few feet ahead of me, beyond a row of shoes neatly lined up at the edge, stretched a massive screen along the floor of the drill hall. It was nearly as wide as the hall, and reached to its midpoint, where it turned in a sharp ninety-degree angle and reared up out of the ground as a massive wall. The entire screen—floor and wall—was flickering in lines of grayscale like a broken 1950s television. This flickering was accompanied by both rhythmic and arrhythmic beats, and by hisses and scratches from a massive, invisible sound system ringing the room.

The screen was bisected down the middle, so that the flicker pattern on the left didn't match up with the flicker pattern on the right. I stood at the center of the edge of the screen, watching one side run up in folds while the other side glitched downwards. Ahead of me, all over the screen in the floor, were barefooted silhouettes, sitting, laying, standing, and far forward, near the base of the great face of the motherboard, I saw one woman dancing.

I added my shoes to the line, trusting I'd find them again eventually, and stepped on to the slightly cool platform in my thin socks. It occurred to me that I did not know what to do at that point. But that is also when I noticed that I still seemed to be moving anyway, as if still on the track I'd switched to when leaving the apartment what felt like hours ago. Not that I was too sure the apartment existed anymore. The sheer scale of The Transfinite was such that I felt completely transported, out of my city, off my planet.

When I entered the hall, the grayscale scroll on each side of the screen had been a tight, rapid flickering, but now it had slowed to a procession—up on the left, down on the right—of large rectangles, black, white, and many shades of grey. The sound reflected this, less frantic now, more solid. Despite all the movement of image and sound, the people seated on the floor-screen upon which I now walked were, for the most part, still and rapt. But I saw that woman still dancing up ahead, a pivoting network of limbs sinuous against a stuttering static background.

I wandered slowly through the seated worshippers, a bit hypnotized, watching the message unraveling along the great face, the thing we had all come here to see, to hear—to witness. It seemed to me to be a sermon. I felt the two hemispheres of my brain pulled in different directions, my whole being bisected as it hooked itself up to this binary interface. Though I was a flesh and blood organism, as were the rest of the congregation, we were able to commune, somehow, with this incomprehensible being.

What was being communicated to us? I struggled to unearth the meaning, to concretize it into words. But there was no use, for if that had been at all possible, "It" would have given us the message in words we could understand, and in Its wisdom, It must have known that we could parse the meaning of its visual glitches and digital yowls. The aural component of the message was relentless, at times a calm triggering of staccato blips over a slightly piercing tone, other times a tremendous rush of bass fuzz and a sound like microphones hooked up to the limbs of nano-bot machines, terrific flutters of an activity somewhere between drilling, welding and swimming, cellular pin-prick sounds magnified to a macro level.

My feet carried me forward, the great wall of visual fuzz rising up taller and taller above me until I took a step forward with my right foot and my toe touched the very base of it. I raised my hands, putting them out slowly, expecting some sort of warmth to radiate off the screen. But the air was as cool as my feet upon the screen on the floor. I was about to touch the wall when a man quietly motioned to me, wearing all the body language of a security guard. I nodded and stepped back.

I let my body sink to the floor and lay down flat, staring up at the scrolling lines of shades of grey as they ticked up and down the two sides of the motherboard's face. With my back against the ground, a swimming feeling rushed through my head, a tryptamine wave riding a rush of fatigue as I surrendered my body to relaxation. The flickering nature of the display invited a trance-like state to come over me. One can go see a painting in a museum and shift weight from one leg to the other, willing oneself to surrender, but the Transfinite hooked me up to its transmission effortlessly. I watched the patches of grayscale climb and fall, felt the buzz and rush of techno-growls vibrating against my skin, resounding through the vast hall.

Lying there for some time, I drifted into a half-sleep, a reverie. The closer I crept to unconsciousness, the more the tryptamine in my system stepped into the foreground, as if it had sunk down from the higher processing units of my brain computer to the background processes that are always running. The hard plasteel floor melted against me and I against it. I threw myself into the science fiction of the motherboard church, imagining that on some intrinsic level, I was being defragmented like any other hard drive.

When I finally sat up, there was a visual buzz to accompany the aural one filling the room, but whereas the sonic element was part of the installation, the visual shake came from me. I sat cross-legged and looked down the length of the screen. The woman was still dancing, and her movements were perfect. The sound booming all around us wasn't what most people would call music, but it's possible to hear music in anything if you listen right—in traffic, in the screams and shouts of a crowd, in the squealing din of a playground—and she heard it here.

I understood her movements, felt them in my own body, and vicariously lived them out through her movements. She was giving herself to the dance completely, oblivious to the staring eyes of those who cared to watch her. Not everyone did. New York City is a place where people grow accustomed to decidedly not watching the unusual. I watched her translate the motherboard's message, bring it down to the level of flesh and blood, from grayscale to Technicolor, from digital to analog.

Then, behind her, I saw a group of people walk past the border of the screen, disappearing behind it. I rose, shakily, the world still all a-buzz, and followed after them. On the flipside of the vertical screen, all was much quieter. The speakers all faced the front of the church, the nave, but back here, there was no such full frontal assault. I walked a ways away from the screen, then turned to look at it.

Code. Math. Language. Written across the screen, scrolling, forming patterns. All of it accompanied by a very simple ticking, like a typewriter or a keyboard, or a small printer. Lines and vectors pierced through the code, forming three-dimensional cartography, a map, all of it printed so as to be understood. The mystery was broken down into mathematical order, understandable to anyone trained in that language. I stood and watched it scroll, erase itself, scroll again. Listening to the sound, echoing from the other half of the chamber, of that mysterious pulsing, glitching song of noise.

So, was that it then? Was it all just zeroes and ones?

Kraftwerk 1 2 3 4 5 6 7 8
Museum of Modern Art
10mg 2c-e

I opened up my pharmacopeia and hovered over the assortment—powders in vials, strips of paper, baggies of plant matter—wiggling my fingers, seeking to divine the right stroke, hone in on the right tool. Tonight, the legendary German techno pioneers Kraftwerk would be performing their clairvoyant 1981 album, *Computer World*, in its entirety in the Marron Atrium of the Museum of Modern Art. It was my intention to not just witness this epic cultural event but to immerse myself in it.

I decided against the tryptamines. They were too earthy, too meaty, too heart-centered, too warm. They might have brought a balanced touch to the icy cyber ecstasies I was hoping to experience, but I didn't want balance this evening. I wanted to throw myself with abandon into the digital moment.

I moved them aside and pored instead over the remaining array of dram vials neatly labeled with coded assortments of letters and numbers. Each of these synthetic mescaline-analog compounds, most of them beginning with the alphanumeric "2C," had its own distinct character—dreamlike, soporific, stark, sensual, abstract, etc. One by one I sifted through them like so many tea leaves until at last there was only one: a glass tube labeled 2,5-dimethoxy-4-ethylphenethylamine, or 2C-E.

We had a checkered history, this molecule and I. It is cold, methodical, analytical, far from the most pleasurable of the materials in my possession, but it can open deep paths of insight. A fellow psychonaut aptly described 2C-E as "challenging material for mature individuals." It has on more than one occasion left me feeling psychologically flayed, and flung far from my humanity, but for *Computer World*, it was the logical choice. I intuited a dose of ten milligrams—enough to enhance, but not overwhelm. Then, I put on a dress shirt and a suit jacket and walked outside.

En route to the museum, I played a game. What if I was an android infiltrating what the science fiction writer William Gibson called meatspace? What if I wasn't a human going to see computer music so much as a computer going to a sort of digital church, to commune with the music of the cybernetic spheres? I moved through Brooklyn streets, through underground tunnels, and rode the rails into Manhattan as the drug very slowly crept into my awareness, pulling the wires of my parasympathetic nervous system taut. I made my movements mechanical. I sat with my hands flat against my thighs, staring straight forward at an empty space on the wall of the subway car. I thought of Blade Runner, of Lieutenant Data, of Isaac Asimov's R. Daneel Olivaw. I thought about computers.

In the MoMA lobby, a cold glass-and-steel feeling splintered through my nervous system. The ticketholders line was abuzz with geeks of every shape and size being herded through a maze of velvet rope. I shuffled with the animals. At each turn we were reminded by walkie-talkie-wielding guards that we must produce our picture identification. I palmed mine, regarding the photo of myself, flattened and broken down into component characteristics. I tilted my head in an affectation of curiosity, emulating a cascade of film and TV androids down through the ages. I looked up and noticed that along the far wall of the lobby, four life-size robotic replicas of the members of Kraftwerk were shifting and pivoting in transparent cubicles, staring blankly ahead.

Once I had been identified, processed, wristbanded and released I made my way up to the atrium. The white walls of the MoMA's architecture grew luminescent, and there was a sheen thickening over everything. As I walked, I felt suspended in a pane of glass through which refracted the most brilliant light. The air became a puddle of gasoline swirled with color. I felt set adrift, and had the distinct sensation that my consciousness was retracting its tentacles from most of my body and climbing inside my spinal vertebrae to center itself entirely in my brain, from which its radiation outward was amplified. The vasoconstriction endemic to the molecule lends itself to a pronounced mind/body duality. My body tightened while my head expanded.

In the atrium I wormed my way to a spot snug in the center of the room, slipping on the 3-D glasses provided for the performance. An eight-channel surround-sound system was rigged around the space. This was the fifth night of a retrospective concert series during which Kraftwerk performed one album per night from its discography. I was one of perhaps four hundred people in the small but airy atrium. The conversations around me blurred into a syncopated din. There was a rhythm to the chatter. There was a beat.

A voice came grinding out of the speakers, familiar, harsh, and metallic. An old digital friend from the days of Speak-and-Spell, with a German accent, artificial intelligence reaching out to make contact.

LAY DEES AND GEN TUL MEN.

KAH – ER – AH – EFF – TAY – VAY – AY – ER - KAH.

The curtain rose on four figures dressed in latex bodysuits patterned with yellow and grey grids, like naked Star Trek holodecks. Each of them stood poised behind a podium, a workstation trimmed with LED lights. The men set about doing…well, what they were doing was not exactly clear. Knobs were perhaps tinkered with, sliders adjusted. The equipment was all concealed. They regarded the crowd dispassionately—not somberly, or harshly, just robotically. The small, enthusiastic crowd cheered.

A digital landscape flooded down around me. Hard, industrial, pounding. Immediately, this was a different *Computer World* than the original recording, which is a creepy but quaint digital artifact. The tone here was deeper, the clangs harsher, the bass heavier. The simplicity of the album's beats was embellished by a staccato attack of machine gun metal. The sounds pierced higher and plunged lower. They weaved farther out of the lanes. The threatening tone, evident but distant in the original recordings, now unveiled itself in all its power.

While the classic cover art to *Computer World* portrayed a type of desktop unit now totally obsolete (floppy drive and all), this take on the album sounded as if it had traveled through many generations of microprocessors, evolving not to keep up with the technology of the times but to harness it. It felt powerful, ominous, defying the obsolescence that makers program into all technology.

The atrium shivered. The 3-D glasses I wore somewhat amputated the rainbow display produced by the drug, but the visuals projected behind the band were enthralling. I felt my self pulled up even further into my head, my eyes swelling out against the red and blue film between them and the world. Despite an instinctive reaction to thudding bass that always seems to insist I dance, I held my body still, as did most people around me. The performers themselves barely moved, their bodies shifting to the music as little as possible. An unspoken agreement swam through the crowd of fashionable nerds that too much movement would be bad form. Throughout the crowd there were some heads bobbing, slight shifts of balance and weight, but mostly people were rapt and still, letting the music work their minds more than their bodies. The synthesizers slid through our ears, technospiritual floss.

My character—the metropolitan android, a cutting edge model built to infiltrate the flesh machines of the city—thrived on this music. The sounds passed through me, rearranging my thoughts into a syncopated simplicity of ones and zeroes. On the screen erected behind the performers, a 3-D representation of computer code streamed past. Voices—male, female, silly, evil, all computerized—recited the numbers one through eight in German, Spanish, Japanese. The song, *Numbers*, passed into the eponymous track, *Computer World*.

My thoughts broke down into simple concepts, gifted to me by the robot voices, the gods I'd come to commune with, my digital overlords. Business. Numbers. Money. People. Business. Numbers. Money. People. The concepts moved like assembly lines through my mind. A vision blossomed behind my forehead of a world irreversibly networked. Communication. Time. Medicine. Entertainment. As I watched the fiber-optic spiderweb weave itself, a sense of wonder and the playful tone of the song gave way to a deeper undercurrent of fear that had been frothing below the surface. The computer voice had more to say, reciting names: Interpol and Deutsche Bank. FBI and Scotland Yard. CIA and KGB. Control the data. Memory. Control the data. Memory. Some of these words kindled small sparks of fear in me, and the agitation brought on by the drug seized upon those sparks and breathed oxygen into them. A nervousness bloomed under my skin, a threat of panic. I could only breathe, listen, and be patient with myself and the drug.

The last track on *Computer World* recites the mantra that "it's more fun to compute," and as I listened to that mantra pounding into my ears, strange reactions churned inside me. The aggressive energy of the 2C-E cut into me, messing with my adopted character's lines and his biography. It can be an incredibly pushy drug, jerking thoughts off-course, dredging up the unwanted. I got all scrambled up. Jolts of crackling intensity writhed along my limbs. I twitched, feeling my joints wound up with energy that needed to be displaced.

The performance of *Computer World* ended, and from there the German robots launched straightaway into a sprawling retrospective of selections from the rest of their discography. The journey oscillated between simple pleasures and dark fears, the latter crystallized most potently in the thick, static-laden, German-accented computer voice reciting a modernized intro to the frightening song "*Radio-activity*:"

> Sellafield 2 will produce 7.5 tons of plutonium every year.
> 1.5 kilograms of plutonium make the nuclear bomb.
> Sellafield 2 will release the same amount of radioactivity
> into the environment as Tschernobyl every 4.5 years.
> One of these radioactive substances, Krypton 85,
> will cause skin cancer and death.

This was followed by a haunting recitation of disaster zones—Tschernobyl, Harrisburg, Sellafield, Hiroshima, Fukushima. Upon hearing the last name, with newsreel images from Japan still fresh in my mind, an immense dread crept through me. All the rainbow shreds and sparkles littering the air seemed to turn against me, hovering like predatory insects with their stingers turned in my direction. The world, a thing once wondrous, was now potent with hostility.

The fear paralyzed me. Through a series of songs that all felt ominous in their own way—*The Robots*, *The Man-Machine*, *Spacelab*—I wrestled with an immense terror that, while I knew it was wholly irrational, utterly consumed me. Everything could go wrong at any moment; the world could implode. And if it did, was I happy? And if I was happy, was that enough? Did I care about more than myself?

It was only when Kraftwerk slipped into the rhythmic, click-and-whirr melodies of their most recent work, the bicycle-inspired Tour de France soundtracks, that fear gave way to lucidity once more. The rhythmic pulse of breath and wheels and road and airstreams blended in my mind, twirling my thoughts into a pleasant daydream. And I felt myself moving.

I could not escape it. The urge to move. The desire to dance. I realized that it had been there all along and that, in my slavishness to playing the part of a robot and to some imagined idea of consensus in the crowd, I had been denying it. So I danced. At first all my movements came in hard angles. I had been holding my body so rigidly that it was not quick to let me ease into movement and lose myself in the flow, but soon I let go of any idea of wrong or right and simply moved.

The more I gave away my body to the pulse of the music, the more I realized something that I had forgotten in the course of a couple of drug-infused hours, something that first fear and now dancing had reawakened: the awareness of the simple, incontrovertible fact of my humanity. As my tendons and muscles stretched and eased into their new regimen of motion, I slipped into a fluidity not just of body but emotion and psyche. As I danced, the fear that still frizzed through my nervous system diffused out into the aether. By the time the curtain fell and the performance ended, I was suffused with light and my body was an engine that churned out joy.

Outside, the Midtown streets were damp. The first raindrops of a thick storm were falling, summoning up that unique smell of wet urban concrete. I listened to and felt the pitter patter against my head and breathed in deeply and walked very slowly to the subway. I let my arms swing and allowed myself to weave down the mostly empty sidewalk, doing little dance steps, hopping first here and then there. At the corner, I performed a completely superfluous and entirely enjoyable spin, doffing an imaginary hat to the sparkling buildings of the city. And I laughed, along the avenue, among the people, and down the subway stairs.

James Turrell
Guggenheim Museum
3mg 5-MeO-MiPT

The James Turrell exhibition at the Guggenheim had spent the summer setting records for attendance at the museum. I was keen to see it, having stumbled upon a retrospective of the artist's work some years back on a visit to Russia. There, my sister and I had wandered the halls as two of perhaps ten or fifteen visitors to Moscow's Garage Center for Contemporary Culture. The works on display had dazzled me with their beauty and their ability to warp my perception through what seemed to be simple yet nuanced tricks of light. I walked out considering myself a fan of Turrell's work.

After slacking all summer in getting to the exhibit at the Guggenheim—the centerpiece of which was a site-specific unique installation titled *Aten Reign*—I made my way to Manhattan's museum mile on the last Sunday before it was to close. I'd had my heart set all summer on exploring a particular phenethylamine—2C-P, known, much like

Turrell's work, for its warping of perception, though where Turrell warped the perception of space, 2C-P was better known for bending one's sense of time.

It seemed almost redundant, however, and I shifted gears. While these experiments I undertake are in the spirit of facilitating a deep engagement with art, the molecules and the intensity of tripping, even at mild doses, can sometimes get in the way. It seemed to make more sense to go another, gentler route. Intuition led me to lift a mostly neglected powder from my collection—5-MeO-MiPT. I find a certain sensual and erotic radiance in the 5-substituted tryptamines that sets them apart from their 4-substituted cousins, a wildness centered in the body. But the dose I prepared myself was incredibly mild. Taking it, I wondered if I would feel anything.

Sunday, September 22nd was the autumnal equinox of the year 2013. The feel of the air outside, cool breezes mixing with hot sun on my skin, had me singing Lou Reed's "Perfect Day" to myself on the way to the subway. Once out, I approached Fifth Avenue from the east and when I turned off 89th St. looking downtown with Central Park on my right and the layered rotunda of the Guggenheim on my left, the song came to mind again. I watched clouds passing over the iconic shell of the museum.

A massive line snaked around the corner and down the length of 88th St. I palmed my American Alliance of Museums card and joined the much shorter members' line, mercifully glad that I had taken a small dose. One got the impression the museum was positively packed, though admission was staggered. The tryptamine began to brush its fingertips against me ever so slightly as I navigated the press of the ticket booths, and then at last I was in.

The lobby of the Guggenheim rotunda looked that day like some cheap contemporary version of a 1960s Be-In. Pillows laid out over the center of the floor were covered in sprawled bodies, and more people lined every inch of the sloping walls, necks and heads and eyes all craned to gaze up at the slowly changing light installation, *Aten Reign*, bleeding down from the distant ceiling through layers of gauzy, nearly transparent white fabric. The din of chatter was overwhelming, and I was reminded, though the smells weren't there, of a shopping mall food court. I decided to save *Aten Reign* for last and made my way first thing to the uppermost floor of the museum where a smaller installation lived. Only a handful of people at a time were admitted to the room to see the piece, and the wait was over an hour long.

I ambled along the line, shuffling when prompted, and lost myself in a book, remembering with a grin just how pleasurable it can be to read when consciousness is so mildly enhanced. I felt an uplift in my mood, a slightly enhanced elasticity of thought, and while the letters on the page remained perfectly still, each word called forth crisp imagery in my mind in a way that felt more visual than conceptual. I was vaguely aware of complaints ahead of me and behind me about the long wait time, but the story I was digging through had me rapt. Before I knew it, I was at the threshold of *Iltar*, which by now had assumed an air of being the most exclusive room of any museum in New York City.

I was two hours past baseline, and I felt cool, collected, and happy. It was not a pushy happiness, as can so often happen with drugs. Rather, it was as if a vibrant, upbeat note in the symphony of my thoughts had been teased out of the lush tapestry of sound to deliver a solo. It was already there, and now it was front and center. I walked into *Iltar*, ready to receive.

A grey rectangle hung on the far wall. On either side of it, two lamps hung down, facing the walls on the left and right of the rectangle respectively. Whereas the line snaking its way through the Guggenheim had been a hotbed of chatter, here everyone was silent, rapt. We stared, through the dim light, at the grey rectangle on the wall. And kept staring.

I stood and stared and allowed my eyes to relax and my face muscles to soften and tuned myself into a receptive state. I stared and received and wondered and never quite became bored but found that I wanted to break the silence, to touch someone around me on the shoulder. We would share a knowing look and say, "Really?"

After ten or fifteen minutes, I walked back down the spiraling rotunda, past the line I had just waited on, which now had grown to twice the length it had been when I'd joined it. I masked my disappointment. Let others experience and decide for themselves. And I would drift back down to *Aten Reign*.

Along the way I stopped to see two more of Turrell's installations. I felt guilty, staring at the rod of light reaching from the ceiling of the corner of a room down to the floor. I supposed I ought to feel something, but even after reading the accompanying texts for a greater understanding of the work, I found myself shrugging, shaking my head.

In another room, a square projection of light in the corner gave the distinct impression of being three-dimensional. When I walked from one side to the other of the room, the angle of the square changed. It was an interesting trick, but it struck me as just that, a trick. A parlor trick, one I thought some friends of mine who put on wild parties in warehouses would not have trouble recreating.

But at least there was *Aten Reign*. I went back down into the rotunda lobby and joined the Be-In, lucking out enough to grab a spot along the bench that ringed the sloping wall. I leaned back, folded my hands behind my head, and gazed up at the radiant conch. I realized I was probably peaking on the 5-MeO-MiPT. So if ever the time was ripe to enjoy a light show, this was it. Colors bled down the walls of the rotunda: peach, turquoise, mauve, violet, orange, bright and heavenly white, ominous and overwhelming red. I lay there for I don't know how long, losing myself in the flux and the shape as best as I could, sharing the space with a throng of others. Laughter, chatter, and the clicking of hundreds of digital shutters filled the space.

In the end, what got me up was the park. The thought of it just across the street kept beckoning me, and I stood up, relinquishing my coveted wall spot to one of the many people standing and leaning back to look up at the piece. As I snaked through the crowd to the exit, I beat myself up, wondering what was different here than the retrospective in

Moscow. Was it all the people? I wondered if I felt "less cool" for being part of something so popular, compared to my previous experience of being alone in a room with a Turrell. Or was I simply unimpressed? I wasn't sure.

It was right of me to leave. I knew it the moment I stepped out on to the sidewalk, and was hit full in the face with the smell and the glory of autumn. The park reared up before me, right across three lanes of Fifth Avenue traffic. I waited for the "walk" sign, crossed the street, and plunged into its leafy embrace. The sour taste of the Turrell exhibit fled in an instant, and back was the sweet song of bliss, echoing in my skull. The park spread out before me, rock and soil and bark and leaf and jogger and bicyclist and dog and man and woman. I slipped into a peripatetic state, following the moment wherever it seemed to lead. Above my head, above the park and all the creatures that thrived within it, the sun burnt a brilliant flame.

On this equinox day, it felt like a curtain call for that blazing soprano of summer. We sang a duet, the sun and I, each in our own radiant way, harmonizing. I walked out into Sheep Meadow, watching massive clouds pass over the soccer players and lovers there, replaced a moment later by the intense glow of the sun's light. Where the shadow of clouds had retreated, now there stretched the long skinny shadows of children over grass as they ran after frisbees. I walked until I found my spot, and anchored myself there, the entire park my Bodhi tree. The shades of green throughout the grass, the glint of skyscraper windows, the sight of my bare feet sprawled out ahead of me after I kicked off my shoes, all delighted me. The light show was incredible. I looked around at the mass of humanity all around me, sharing in the joy of green leaves and public space, and knew that I not only loved them, but that I loved to share this with them.

I lay back, closing my eyes, watching the strange shapes that played behind my eyelids, which had nothing to do with the tryptamine and everything to do with biology. I said a silent thanks for the day, even for going to an exhibit so overwhelmingly disappointing. I had a newfound appreciation for that great giver of life and light hanging in the firmament.

Om: At Giza
The Metropolitan Museum of Art
15mg 4-HO-DiPT

As is the case on every summer day, tourists perched and fluttered like birds along the regal steps leading up to the Metropolitan Museum of Art. It's a picture that has come to seem as much a part of the museum as any of the relics and masterpieces inside. I crossed Fifth Avenue, taking in the scene as I walked towards the hallowed institution's marble staircase, skirting around street performers and food vendors.

New York City lay in the thrall of a massive, archetypal heat wave, but the crowd out in front of the Met was still thick. All the colors of the rainbow were represented in the garb of the people who sat and stood along the steps, fanning themselves and chatting. The heat and the colors and the din mixed with the cloying scent of cotton candy and the upbeat music blasting out of a tinny boom-box behind a pair of breakdancers all gave the scene a carnivalesque feel.

But then, I was feeling rather "silly" myself. I had known that I wanted to trip for this evening's concert, but I wasn't feeling up to any sort of deep plunge into psychospiritual realms. Once any trip I took was over, I'd need to return home and pack for a very early flight the next day. So I'd prepared myself a dose of a compound that I had tucked away for special occasions such as this, and I had taken it just as I was leaving home.

As Sasha Shulgin notes in his tryptamine opus *TiHKaL*, 4-HO-DiPT is quite possibly the fastest-acting, shortest-lasting tryptamine yet discovered, when taken orally at least. Its brief duration—sometimes up and down within the space of just two or three hours—plus the light-hearted uplift of mood it engenders make it an ideal enhancer for concerts or films. The dose-response curve is steep, however, so that the slightest uptick in dosage can push it into much more profound dimensions where, despite its brief duration, it can be almost punitively intense.

I felt the buoyant onset of the drug's effects, perhaps kickstarted by the epic scope of the building spreading across my view. I climbed upwards. Scattered throughout the colorful tourists all up and down the Met's broad staircase was a motley assortment of men and women who seemed comparatively out of place, as if aliens had beamed a bunch of concertgoers up from a heavy metal show and transported them here. So next to families in brand new "I HEART NY" shirts with cameras around their necks I saw pale-skinned people with gauges in their ears wearing black shirts with variations of necrotic imagery—skulls, thorns, mythic beasts, and words steeped in the vocabulary of darkness.

I knew why they were there; though I was dressed in khaki shorts and a plain purple t-shirt, I was one of them. I peered through the shimmering haze rising off the steps and the street, searching out my companion. He tapped me on the shoulder from behind. We headed into the museum and I handed him a ticket. "OM: At Giza," read the text printed across it.

It was close to six in the evening, and most of the foot traffic in the museum was headed outwards. We joined in with a smaller stream headed in, towards the Egyptian collection in the Sackler Wing, which has housed the ancient Temple of Dendur for the past thirty-five years. The Met had hosted performances of gentle classical pieces there in the past, but only very recently had they warmed to the idea of having electrified rock bands play the room.

For OM, an experimental stoner drone trio based out of San Francisco, it was a dream come true. One of their seminal releases, *The Conference of the Birds* (named after a very famous, ancient, Persian mystical allegorical poem), features a fifteen minute long epic piece titled "At Giza," which would be the centerpiece of the night's performance, performed mere feet away from an actual Egyptian temple. OM's music is steeped, beginning with the band's name itself, in spiritual themes, often using elements of Byzantine chant and the repetition of mantras.

The ticket I had handed my companion was a hot one—the performance was one night only, and as we joined the line of tattooed attendees, the excitement in the air was palpable. I stood with my friend in the line, which curled through hallways of the Egyptian wing, past artifacts of stone and lapis lazuli, the carved faces of pharaohs staring blankly and sagely ahead, sphinxes and birds and cats all around us.

Conversation came easily enough, though the tryptamine kept pushing upwards, so that I would catch my breath, expecting to be plunged all of a sudden into much deeper realms but finding that once the hiccup passed, I was still here, breathing, listening. Joy fluttered through me, anchored in nothing but the physical reality of my existence.

The longer I looked at the people all up and down the line, the more I realized how non-homogenous the crowd really was. OM's music touches on so many themes that they seemed, in fact, to have pulled a fascinating cross-section of human beings to see them, music fans stretching the gamut from hippie to nerd to metalhead. Dreadlocked hippie goddesses mingled with polo-shirt wearing record store clerks while flat-brim cap-wearing hip hop kids waited just ahead of them.

The line snaked past pharaoh heads that looked like cobras, and eventually we came into the rhomboid room that houses the Temple of Dendur. A reflecting pool, symbolic of the river Nile, stretches across the entrance. One entire wall is constructed of glass and slopes downward at an angle, allowing sunlight to flood the room. We made our way around the pool, up towards the space in front of the temple itself where the stage had been erected. I was disappointed to see that the stage faced the temple, where it would serve as a muse to the band, but be at the backs of the audience.

The temple itself always surprises me; I expect it to be bigger, grander. But it is a simple structure made up of two distinct pieces. The first, the gateway to the temple, is a tall rectangular doorway, covered all over in hieroglyphics. Set a bit farther back from the doorway is a squatter structure, the temple proper, which is less intricately decorated. Two columns frame the entrance to an offering hall where sacrifices were once made, long ago, when the temple stood in the Nile valley.

The early evening summer sun slanted down through the sloped glass wall and filled the room to brimming with brightness. It didn't feel quite right. Knowing the heavy rumbling bass drone that runs through OM's music, and the dark tones that suffuse it, I found myself wishing it was the middle of winter, when by six o'clock darkness would have lain thickly over the city. The crowd aggregated around the stage; my friend and I hung back, near the periphery. I felt a continuous lifting now, as if tiny invisible wings were pushing me up from the undersides of my arms, my legs, my eyelids. My thoughts took flight as well. My mind filled with random fantastical free associations, but every breath grounded me once more in the temple space.

OM took the stage to a very personal sort of applause from the crowd. It was the type of reception one expects from an audience that feels deeply connected and committed to an artist, very different from the screaming of the legions at pop concerts in stadiums. The crowd of seasoned fans knew that this was an epic moment for the band, and was proud to be there with them. Though I wasn't that die-hard a fan of OM's, my porous boundaries made me sensitive to the ambient energy of the crowd and I was swept up into it. Surrounded by sacred architecture and touched by the tryptamine, I got the feeling that I might be standing on the doorstep of something approaching revelation.

The three-piece ensemble ambled into a slow building drone. Rushes of softly played cymbals blended with gently thumped hand drums while the bass guitar trundled through the deepest reaches of the low end. Singer and bassist Al Cisneros held space on stage like a behemoth, his massive form holding the bass like an extension of his own body, fingers jumping from fret to fret. I trained all my focus on the music, on the twists of the players' faces, on the drama unfolding from the speakers.

For as long as I could. When Cisneros began to sing, a low droning that slipped in and out of his own bass lines with words I could only barely make out, the dramatic element was ratcheted up, but I felt left behind. Part of it was merely volume: an OM show is typically of the deafening variety, and the band was undoubtedly playing as loud as the Metropolitan Museum of Art's board of directors would allow them to, but it wasn't quite loud enough for them to find their groove. If the band's sound engineers had had their way, I'm sure dust would have been flaking off the ruins behind me.

I turned to face those ruins, and the shift in perspective completely transformed my experience of the room and the music. The music fell into the background, swimming around and behind my ears, flowing through the space around the temple. The sun was setting, but slowly; we weren't far past the solstice in the calendar, and it would likely be light out even when we left the concert, but the color was changing hues. The light in the room had been a piercing whitish yellow, but as the sun sank closer to the tops of distant skyscrapers, its light broke apart as through a prism, traversing gradients of red, ruddy orange, and a spectrum of citrusy yellows. The light caught the temple, illuminating the hieroglyphics scrawled over its surface. Some of these symbols had of course been eroded by time and weather, but many still remained surprisingly crisp and clear.

I watched the temple in the light, over the heads of the crowd sprawled out around the stage, becoming aware at times that the spectators' heads were bouncing up and down more than before, that there was an enhanced intensity to the sound swelling from the band. When I looked over, they were in the throes of what felt like an ancient Persian war-song, a slide guitar singing out exotic tones to flicker around the aggressive sludge of drum and bass that were trying so hard to thunder through the speakers as much as was allowed.

The drummer sat drenched in sweat, casting a ravenous gaze on the cymbals before he hit them. The multi-instrumentalist who switched back and forth from percussive to string instruments seemed to be in an ecstatic Sufi trance state. And the bassist/singer lumbered in place, lips moving slightly as if whispering to himself, eyes rolling back in his head as he drove the low rumble of his bass through the sand.

I had no doubt that these men were engaged in what was to them a spiritual practice, that the music they were making was a vehicle not just for expression but for catharsis and communion. A deep longing and pain rode the sound waves, that much I could not deny, but ultimately something about the drama of it, the heaviness of it, struck me as just so much artifice.

After a few songs, drummer and bassist left the stage while the multi-instrumentalist stayed behind, singing with plaintive, gorgeous longing into a microphone. Without the rhythmic noise around him, I found the sound haunting and beautiful, but he was rejoined soon enough by his bandmates and they struck up the opening notes to the centerpiece of the evening, the 20-minute long epic "At Giza."

I stood there, still hoping the tips of my toes were at the threshold of a potential doorway to revelation, but I took a step back, withdrawing from the crowd so tuned into the amplified priests on stage. I wandered off from my companion through the loose fringes of the crowd at its edges. A cool stone bench ringed the space and I sat upon it, running my fingers against the smooth stone. A few yards away sat the Temple of Dendur.

As a child I had dreamed of cavorting with the gods of myth, partaking in their dramas. I fantasized about traveling to the Hall of Ma'at where Anubis would weigh my heart against a feather to see if I was worthy of eternal afterlife. While the mythmakers on the stage across from the temple continued on their journey, I found myself focused on the dilapidated simplicity of the temple sitting right before me. If it was anything, it was real. Its sandstone bore marks both natural and manmade. On the one hand the two structures were covered with writing, and both were natural substances molded to human purpose by human will, but both had been worn away by wind and dust and floods. I couldn't touch them, of course, so I just opened my gaze to them, while rubbing my fingers against the stone of my seat.

OM had a small light show set up on stage: simple reds, whites and blues were used to illuminate them, and only sparingly, since the sun was still up when the show began. But as "At Giza" drew closer to its conclusion they were used more, since the bronze rays of the sun were slipping farther and farther from view. I watched the band, and then noticed something on the wall beyond them. As the light slanted lower and lower, it came down through the sloping glass wall behind me to land upon the reflecting pool at the entrance to the vast space.

The symbolic Nile was glittering. I saw, when I looked over, that the water in it was moving ever so slightly and where peaks and meniscuses would rise, they caught the last of the evening light and reflected and refracted it up against the wall across from me, so that liquid lines of light were splayed across it, writhing slowly. As "At Giza" grew in intensity, the sun fell lower, and the liquid light worms rose higher, and when the band droned out its final tones, the light remained, quivering.

I rejoined my companion and we walked a circuit of the temple, and gazed with smiles upon the stone sarcophagi set off to one side, etched with images from head to toe. That rhythmic upward lift I had felt was now settling me down instead in pulses, gently. We passed back through hallways full of artifacts and out into the stifling heat that persisted even as the sun set over Fifth Avenue. I felt my normally gregarious nature enhanced and relished all the exchanges of ideas that passed between us as we walked to the subway. It was now three hours since I'd swallowed the capsule of 4-HO-DiPT, and by the time the train deposited me in Brooklyn I was for all intents and purposes sober.

When I turned on the light in my apartment and my cat came bounding at me, I perceived with fresh eyes how the lamp I turned on every day illuminated patterns and whorls in the hardwood floor and other things I hadn't really noticed before. I left the stereo off and sat on my sofa, listening to the creak of the building, the sounds of life outside, the low hum of the refrigerator. I watched the lamplight bouncing into cracks and caroming off of surfaces of wood and metal and plastic. I looked around at the artifacts of my life, my tchotchkes and mementos and papers and scraps, all the things I held on to, hanging around my apartment like mirrors, and I felt just a bit like an archaeologist.

The Forty Part Motet
The Cloisters Museum
1.7g psilocybe cyanescens

It was the kind of Sunday morning that calls for mushroom tea. Unpredictable shifts and swings in climate had cheated New York of all but a couple of weeks of fall in recent years, but now a particularly rich and lush autumn bathed the city.

My stomach quivered a bit as I crushed the dried mushrooms into smaller pieces, placing them in a mesh tea ball, as if my whole organism were alive with muscle memory. They were beautiful mushrooms of the species psilocybe cyanescens. A friend had picked them in the forests of the Pacific Northwest and carried them across the country before gifting them to me. I thought of him with gratitude.

I steeped the mushrooms with a bag of rooibos tea for fifteen minutes, adding a slice of lemon, then poured the concoction into a thermos and headed for the subway. It was a long ride from the heart of Brooklyn up to the northern tip of Manhattan. I rumbled along underground for a little over an hour, sipping at the tea slowly, finishing it over the course of the first twenty minutes of the ride.

The effects came on in waves—gentle but urging. Nausea crept over me, but in a way I enjoyed it. I rarely eat mushrooms anymore, but I had been sitting in ayahuasca ceremonies somewhat regularly the past few years, and as the onset of the mushrooms set my guts to roiling, I had a different perspective on that sick feeling than I once had. Though I knew there were biochemical, physiological reasons for my nausea, it seemed evident to me from experience that the medicine I had taken was interfacing with my organism, communicating with it, and I only had to give myself over to the discomfort in order to pass through it.

It was easy enough. I'd recently acquired a marvelous collection of music titled *I Am The Center*, issued by a boutique record label out of Seattle called Light in the Attic Records. The collection anthologizes obscure private-issue "new age" music from America between the years 1950 and 1990, mining a rich history of self-published experimental music handmade on analog equipment. When my whole being began to tingle, I slipped headphones into my ears and pressed play on the first disc. The many faces of Manhattan walked in and out of the subway car as it headed north, but they were now accompanied by gongs, flutes, chants and synthesizers.

Besides the musical accompaniment, I felt hale and prepared for the trip. I'd spent the last couple of months tuning into healthier modes of living, learning for the first time in my life the value of good sleep and making changes to diet and lifestyle that had me feeling as if all the gears inside were clicking and whirring in good order. So as the mushrooms came on, I didn't feel I had anything to run from.

I exited at 190th Street and headed into Fort Tryon Park, my thoughts swimming in the etherea of the music. Fort Tryon Park has always seemed to me to have less defined landscaped boundaries than the other major parks of New York I am familiar with. Space wasn't carved out for the park so much as the park defined its own space, and the city grew around it. There's still a deep sense of wildness in parts of that park. There are twists and turns along sheer faces of rock, with the Hudson River running below, and the imposing cliffs of the Palisades in New Jersey on the far shore, across the water, adding a dramatic element to the vistas. One can forget the city entirely…for a little while at least.

Wind strummed the trees as a harp sang in my ears, many of the notes quarter-tones that set an off-kilter vibe to my steps that perfectly suited the soft rush of the trip. The onset had lost its edge and now in its place I felt a continuous lifting propelled by each inhalation of crisp autumn air. That same air nipped at any skin I had exposed—fingers poking out of gloves, my neck where my scarf hung open, my face—and made me conscious of my own warmth, of the blood coursing through me. I walked much slower than my usual rat race pace, awestruck by the sheets of autumnal color hanging from the immense trees rising up all around me.

I descended a flight of steep stone steps, following signs to the Heather Gardens. I'd never noticed that pathway before, had always gone along a different route. I followed a path high along the river, then turned into the Gardens. It was like stepping into an illustrated fairy tale book.

I've never been one to point out flora by name. I love the sound of words like "asphodel" and "hydrangea" and "rhododendron," but I couldn't possibly point them out. So the Gardens weren't a collection of species to me so much as fields of color. And how many there were. I must have come on a perfect day, I thought, since every color of the spectrum was represented in the tiers and tufts of plants and flowers. The only dullness came from the sky, where an unbroken rippling sheet of grey cloud cover stretched from horizon to horizon. I wandered along the uppermost path through the Gardens, looking for a bench to call my own for a time, when rain began to fall.

A light wind picked up, throwing sprays of rain down on the stone pathways and the florid leaves that were clinging to whatever spectrum of light they could hold on to, red, orange, purple, yellow. I scurried out of the Gardens, following the signs to the Cloisters, seeing hints of its high stone walls rising in the distance.

The final approach was lined with massive trees that had lost half their foliage, the pathway beneath them lined with crunchy masses of dead leaves. As I walked under them, with ethereal voices chanting "Om Mani Padme Hum" in my ears over a soft ambling piano, I looked up at the naked limbs reaching out to the sky holding nothing, their offerings fallen to death.

A memory came back to me of my friend Margaret, who had died of cancer some years ago. I'd visited her in hospice on the day before she died. She had been a dancer in her youth and the last that I had seen of her that day, she had sat up in her bed, looked at us gathered around her, and slowly held out her arm and flexed her hand and fingers, posing with a heart-wrenching dancer's grace. Suddenly all the trees were Margaret, dead, dying, reaching out.

Sanskrit chanting gave way to a droning hum, an eerie tune that matched the wind and precipitation whipping about under the vast grey blanket in the sky. I stood overlooking the river and the Palisades across the way, a smile writ on my face as light sheets of moisture washed over me. It was difficult to care about getting soaked when the moment was so beautiful. I couldn't turn my back on it. But when the current track ended and the drone gave way to a soft, playful tinkling of electronic bells, I did.

The Cloisters reared up in the distance, a medieval castle nestled in a forest. I shook off my reverie and hustled through the rain to the entranceway, a magnificent cochlear spiral cobblestone path. The Cloisters had seemed a solid grey from a distance, but as I walked up closer to the structure, I saw that the stones were a mottled mix of grey and light pastel colors, tan and peach and beige, giving the impression of a zoomed-in view of a mosaic.

Just before I crossed the threshold into the museum, a squirrel so black as to be midnight blue scampered across my path. I watched it scurry away from me for a few yards, and then it stopped, sat back on its haunches and cocked its head. Then it turned and stared at me. We eyed one another like that while rain and wind beat against us. I flinched, blinked, lost the contest, and it was gone. The first disc of music ended. I put my headphones away, and entered the museum.

When I visit the Cloisters, it's more about the journey, the park, and the architecture than seeing the works of art housed there, all of which hail from medieval Europe. But this trip was undertaken to experience one work in particular. For the first time in the Cloisters' 75-year history, a contemporary art piece was on display within its walls. Janet Cardiff, a Canadian artist, had set up her sound installation "The Forty Part Motet" in a chapel within the Cloisters. Though the piece centers on a recording of religious classical music, it had never before been exhibited in a religious space.

I made a beeline for the Fuentidueña Chapel where it was set up. The crowd was thicker than I had expected for a rainy Sunday and the majority of people there were headed in the same direction. I skimmed the infographic at the entrance to the chapel. The installation was a recording of a choir performing a reworking of a complex mid-16th Century piece titled *Spem in alium numquam habui* by the Tudor composer Thomas Tallis. The title translates to "in no other is my hope." The recording would last eleven minutes and be repeated all day, with a three-minute spoken word interlude in between each round.

I stepped into the chapel, a long stone chamber with high, airy ceilings. An oval of forty hi-fidelity speakers ringed the space, reaching from the doorway to the far end of the elevated nave. All the speakers faced inwards. Copper audio wiring laced down their stands to the floor, reaching out to the walls of the chapel where they were braided together in thick ropes like golden veins.

Where a step led up to the nave at the far end of the chapel, a large wooden carving of the crucified Jesus hung, suspended from the ceiling. A crown sat upon his head and light gilding work was trimmed along the hem of the cloth about his waist and the edges of the large cross to which he was nailed. His facial expression was sad, but not resigned.

I heard no music, but straining my ears I couldn't hear any spoken word interlude either. I shifted weight from foot to foot, distracted suddenly by my own stillness and the force of the trip rushing through me, within and without, amplified now by my lack of motion. I wasn't dispelling any of that energy into activity and it turned me restless.

Then an alto voice rose to fill the void, somewhere behind me and off to the right. I turned my attention towards the speaker from which it originated, when a band of sopranos joined the chorus from far across the chapel, sounding from the nave behind Christ. Tenors joined their throats to the chorus, then baritone and bass, so that in the blink of an eye the nature of the space and all within it was completely transformed, the audience swept up and enmeshed in a tapestry of human sound flowing from the speakers all around.

I was standing somewhat close to one speaker and I heard the voice of a single tenor. More than heard it. It enveloped me, swam into me, joined with the air that I was breathing. I felt every atom in my body vibrating.

As the sound rang through and around me, I surveyed the crowd gathered in the chapel. Some were young, some were old, some seemed like secular folks brought here by ravenous aesthetic appetites, while others had their heads bowed and their hats in their hands in pious devotion. And surely there were others like me, navigating a gray space somewhere between belief and the lack of it, immersing themselves in experience.

The man upon the cross, who hung in the center of this entire swelling chorus of thundering, sweeping invocation meant little to me. I certainly didn't see him as my savior. If anything, I saw him as a tragic example of what often happens to people with notions that run contrary to those of the powers that be. I looked around the chapel, and felt the rush of history: a man had died upon a cross, and the fervent belief of some who followed him changed the course of history.

I was thinking with great sadness of the careening wreck of fundamentalist religious thought, of all the atrocities, murders, wars waged in the name of gods by men, when I realized that I had tears upon my cheeks. I wiped at them in wonder, sniffling, and noticed that I wasn't alone in crying. Quite a few people in the chapel were so moved.

How strange to weep over the religious prayers of an ancient, somewhat creepy death cult. And yet I was. The voices poured forth as one being, swirling through the space and the people gathered there as a flock of birds moves through the sky. Twice the chorus died to silence, then built up into soft rivers once more. I thought of Bach and

Beethoven, the sculptures of Rodin, all the Christian art and artists that had so moved me, a secular Jew, for all my life, while I stared up at the strange face of Jesus Christ upon the cross.

Spem in alium ended. Somewhat abruptly, the voices all joined together for one unified note held in space and time and then all of them simply died away. An uncomfortable silence fell over the chapel and many people shuffled towards the exit. I wiped the last tears from my eyes and waited for the spoken word interlude. I had thought, on my way up, that I would listen to the piece many times since it was so short, but now I couldn't imagine sullying that first listen with successive ones. I waited for the interlude, but nothing came.

I thought I heard a sound emitting from one of the nearby speakers, low and indistinct. I walked close and put my ear to the speaker and heard the voices of small children. It was as if they were playing with toys. "The red one," I heard, "and the blue too, no not that one!" I could hear the voices of adults further in the distance, wherever they were. I looked around at the people still remaining in the chapel, but no one else seemed to hear it. I wondered if it was some weird sort of cell phone interference with this speaker, or if perhaps some of the speakers were wired up to another part of the museum for the so-called interlude.

I was wondering all these things when one of the children's voices became much clearer in the speaker. He said, with a slight lisp, "This is Janet Cardiff's *Spem in alium*" and the speaker fell quiet for a few heartbeats, and then the Forty Part Motet began again. The crowd in the chapel was half the same people as the last round and half a new bunch. I moved towards the nave, wanting to experience the piece from another perspective entirely, forgetting all my ideas of only hearing it once.

It was no less beautiful on the second round but try as I might—since I love a good cry—I couldn't summon up that first emotional reaction. Gone was the immediate response of the heart, and in its place was only a pure aesthetic appreciation of the texture of the voices and the way they each joined, complemented, and interwove with the others. I had a more "detached observer" perspective on the installation. I was re-experiencing it with less wonder and a more critical ear.

When it ended once again, I leaned in close to a speaker near my new spot. Two men with British accents were discussing *Spem in alium*, one of them saying that he had last heard it performed live in the U.S.S.R. almost twenty five years earlier. "Ah, yes, is that right?" said his friend, and suddenly I understood. The children in the other speaker were sopranos, and these were adult singers, perhaps tenors judging from their speaking voices. I moved from one speaker to the next, listening to recordings of the chatter of the choir between takes of recording.

When the piece began again for a third time, I was in a new position, flanked by sopranos. I gazed up at Jesus and swept my gaze across the field of people. There were a handful I recognized from the first two listens and many more new faces. I counted three or four people lifting their faces in prayer to their savior, their lips moving even as the choir sang all around them. But he seemed so much less powerful to me, and to me that was the brilliance in the interlude. The recording was exceptionally beautiful, but I knew this would be my last time listening to it, and as I listened to it something shifted in my appreciation. I felt the awareness not of the target of the singing—God—but an awareness of the voices' origins. Throats and lungs and minds. These were human sounds.

It ended, and I made my way for the exit. I told myself not to listen to any more of the interlude, lest I get swept into a fourth round, but I couldn't resist. I leaned in close to a speaker and heard the choirmaster this time, giving instruction to some of the singers. Then I slipped out the chapel door. As I made my way down the stone hallway towards the exit, I heard the choir take up the song once more, off in the distance behind me.

The rain had passed. While that grey sheet of cloud still stretched across the sky, it was thinner now, wispier, and in the distance it was peeling back to reveal a bright pale blue. And where the sun hung above the clouds, I could see a spot of brightness begging to be revealed. I walked down a stone path, putting my headphones in my ears, and sat on a bench overlooking the river and the distant tree-lined New Jersey shore.

For the next hour I sat and listened to soft sounds, the second half of *I Am The Center*, while meditating on the pins of light caught in the ripples of the Hudson and the multicolored foliage on the opposite shore. A hawk hung in the air for what seemed an impossibly long time, hovering in one place like a kite stuck in a tree, somehow riding a jet stream of air in perfect stillness.

At one point a tension seemed to take hold of the sky. The cloud cover was peeling back with aching slowness. As the electronic symphony of sounds in my ears slowly built higher and higher, the grey sheath peeled further and further apart until, just as the song was exploding into its most joyous tones, the sun revealed itself in blinding glory. I held my hand up to soften its dazzling radiance, peeking through my fingers and letting myself be blinded just enough to bask in its beauty, repeating over and over: wow.

As it slipped out from behind the clouds, the sun was also setting, and it wasn't long before the bench beneath me grew much colder and set a chill into my limbs. I ambled back towards the Heather Gardens, passing under the trees that danced like Margaret. At one point I stopped, stepped off the paved pathway into the trough of fallen dead leaves that ran along beside it, and resumed my walking. I watched with an unfettered smile while leaves of orange and red and yellow and brown kicked up with my every step like fireworks.

I wove through the paths of the Gardens for a bit, wanting to listen to the rest of the album before I got on the subway to go home. The last song was made of three different types of sounds. The first was the rush of running water. The second was a very softly played piano. And the third was a single human voice, echoing, calling gently in sound without words. It touched something inside me, that voice, and for a moment I felt a pulse of raw emotion welling up in me like it had in the chapel. I stood in the cold and watched the sun slip down until the song ended.

Dia:Beacon
Hudson River Valley
32mgs TMA-2

I had worked the timing out perfectly. Based on previous experiences with TMA-2, one of Alexander Shulgin's earliest phenethylamine creations, I knew what to expect from the onset: it would be long, slow, gradual. I took the dose, thirty-two milligrams—about twenty milligrams shy of what I might take in the comfort of my own home—before leaving my apartment for the subway. By the time I boarded a northbound train leaving New York City in approximately one hour, it would just start to kick in.

Unfortunately, my faith in the MTA was misplaced, a lesson every New Yorker regularly learns anew. The express train ran local, dawdling at each station while the conductor's voice came through tinny speakers begging patience. By the time I bounded up the stairs into palatial Grand Central Terminal, I'd already missed the 11:43 AM Poughkeepsie-bound train. The next train to Beacon wouldn't depart for an hour. I hooked my thumbs in my backpack's straps and took a deep breath, noting how every solid surface seemed a bit more active, a bit more vibratory. I felt hyper-aware of my legs.

Standing still in the midst of the commotion of the terminal's main hall made me dizzy. Hundreds of passengers and their well-wishers murmured along, taking photographs, consulting schedules, rushing for their trains. Motion seemed to be the rule of the game, so I decided to keep moving, seeing if I could displace the nervous stirring energy of the molecule's onset.

Marble steps carried me up to a balcony overlooking the central hall, a perch that gave me more sense of control as everything loosened. The late winter sun slanted weakly through the iron grates covering the massive southerly-facing windows, so that despite the electric blue brightness outside the marble surfaces all around, the chandeliers, globes, and the iconic golden clock atop the information booth at the center of the concourse were all suffused with soft yellow light.

Grand Central Station isn't the worst place to be stranded for an hour. The city has many different hearts, depending on your perspective and your purpose at any given time, but this, the central rail hub for the Metro North railway and a handful of subway lines, is certainly one of them. Standing in this monumental relic of a gilded age beneath the huge mural of constellations painted across the high arched ceiling in tasteful tones of gold leaf and green, I always get a sense of humanity reaching far above itself. I've always been partial to Grand Central for the same reason I am fond of elegant bridges—they are cathedrals of connection that celebrate the scurrying of human beings to and fro.

I was experiencing classic psychedelic time dilation, but I was able to snap out of my reverie, check the clock at the center of the concourse and find that my next train was leaving soon. I found my track and, having taken this train before and being familiar with the views it offers, searched out a seat along a western-facing window. Once settled, the relief of motion quickly fled, and the undeniable weirdness of the drug came on in juddering waves as I settled against the vinyl upholstery. I felt keenly aware of my skull and teeth and a general queasy tremor rolled through my limbs, so that I paradoxically felt very aware of my skeleton and as if I were made of nothing but churling liquid.

I'd picked TMA-2—trimethoxyamphetamine-2—because my feelings about it lined up quite nicely with the feelings I had about my destination. I was on a northbound train that would drop me off in Beacon, NY, where a 300,000 square foot former Nabisco box factory had been turned, some forty years earlier, into an airy, light-filled, contemporary art museum by the Dia Art Foundation. Dia:Beacon is a regular pilgrimage site for me: I wind up there two or three times a year, and its permanent collection by turns astonishes and confounds me. Some pieces I love with all of my heart, and some I can't stand. This is typical of many people's reactions to modern art. I feel much the same about TMA-2, a feeling succinctly summed up by a fellow traveler in one of our sessions: "This is very strange. Uncomfortable, not exactly enjoyable, but, I am having the greatest time."

The compact city exhaled the train out into the Bronx and beyond, past an ugly twist of highway overpasses and the sprawling urban edge. A massive billboard read "GRATTITUDE" in block letters.

City gave way to suburb gave way to countryside as the train pulled alongside the Hudson River. As the landscape expanded on both sides of the train, I felt myself loosening up as well. Where before all I had seen were right angles and tall slabs of concrete and glass, now there was the rush of a river and hills dotted with the leafless limbs of not-yet-spring.

The chopped face of rock across the Hudson stretched on and on, like the cross-section of one massive felled log. As the train chugged farther north, a winter more beautiful and lovable than the harsh urban freeze of the past few months showed its face to me. Much of North America had endured a brutal winter and even now, in the middle of March, it abated only with agonizing slowness. Leaving the city behind me and traveling up into a different kind of winter with fields instead of skyscrapers, I felt as if I were expanding out beyond my skin, across hills still dappled with untrammeled snowfalls, the lifelessness of barren trees offset by the vivid refraction of sunlight on the crystalline snow. Occasional evergreens sprayed welcome bursts of green into the otherwise dead scenery.

The walk from the Beacon railway station to Dia is short, curling along a footbridge and wending alongside a brief stretch of the local main road, leading eventually into a parking lot that looks like the yard of any corporate headquarters in America, with a low building in the distance stretching out long and wide towards the horizon. It is easy to imagine, upon arriving, the coming and going of factory workers in days gone by. Being familiar with the layout of the museum, I had nascent ideas as to how I wanted to spend this altered time. I had a couple of hours until the museum closed. I walked down the spacious main hallway that extends from the entranceway, treading the wooden floorboards past massive walls on either side of me on which were mounted irregular shapes, each painted a single striking hue. *24 Colors—(For Blinky)*, the German artist Imi Knoebel's homage to his deceased friend and mentor Blinky Palermo, has always reminded me of the bowl of candy that sat on the table in the waiting room of my childhood pediatrician—a comforting, completely non-threatening feast of color. A couple walked down the same hall, further along, and their young child squealed in delight as he wheeled about in every which direction, surrounded by what must have seemed like confetti or giant marshmallows.

I turned right and wended my way into the maze of massive line drawings by the artist Sol LeWitt (though it is my understanding that LeWitt simply comes up with the guidelines for these line drawings, then metes out the grunt work to his students…). At first glance these works seem like they would be right up my alley, a few of them being mindbending matrices, but they have always bored me, seeming like little more than glorified doodles.

I stood before one of the most complicated of these drawings and relaxed the tension that gripped my nervous system. The drug's presence was flooding into me now, and there was no damming its energy, but I breathed into it and made a conscious effort to stand tall, square my shoulders, and relax weight evenly through my body. I relaxed my face muscles, softened my gaze, and dove into LeWitt's drawing. I couldn't help but smile as the lines twisted all out of place, no longer fixed on the surface of the wall but writhing instead. And rather than simply threads of black against a white surface, all sorts of radiant color seemed to be shimmering just off the edges of each individual line.

"Cool," my inner monologue said, barely leaving off a dopey, "man" at the end of it. I shook my head. This was just too easy. There was no way I could get a clear read on work like LeWitt's in this state of mind. I couldn't praise it and I couldn't damn it—the drug was just too distracting, and the visual perturbations around the edges of the work still struck me as nothing more than a parlor trick. I kept moving.

Next door, a cavernous rectangular space was ringed, with no breaks between them except for two doorways, with prints from an Andy Warhol series called *Shadows*. Seventy-two canvases varying, in typical Warhol fashion, on a theme—the same two images, portrayed in different colors, many distinctly Day-Glo. While I've always appreciated Warhol as a countercultural figure and a presence in recent American history and identity, his art has never really gripped me in any way. I walked in one door of the *Shadows* room and towards the other, but without even realizing it, found myself turning around at the far end and swinging in a circle around the circumference of the room, mesmerized by the way the two images repeated ad nauseum in different coloring seemed so very different from one another.

The museum was busier than I expected on a Sunday, and to my simultaneous delight and chagrin, many of the attendees were incredibly beautiful women with impeccable fashion sense. TMA-2 has a mighty body load, and though it can be overwhelming and not always pleasant (and often nauseating) it is a body load that brings with it a great rush of sensuous feeling and the awakening of all sorts of erotic energies. I steered past a group of French girls chatting in their native tongue and felt neon fires dancing through my limbs, then steered myself towards the nearest piece of art I could find in order to ground myself.

At this point I wondered if perhaps I had misjudged a museum dose of this particular substance. My brow was damp with sweat and the breadth of experience, of overloaded senses, spiraling thoughts, hypersensitivity to people and their smells and sounds, deepened and deepened and showed no sign of relenting. I saw a couple down the hall ahead of me laughing as they looked into a room, then walk away shaking their heads. I made a bee-line for it.

Inside that small room, a group of wooden chairs stood in a circle, facing inwards towards one another. They were plain wooden chairs, thick and sturdy. The space in the middle of all the chairs was empty, and yet I was struck by what seemed to be an immense presence in the room. I had expected, from the laughter of the people checking out the exhibit before me, to scoff at yet another piece of what I thought was pretentious art. I wondered why I didn't find this pretentious. After all, it was just a bunch of chairs. Arranged in a circle. Couldn't anyone do that?

Titled *The Pure Awareness of the Absolute*, the space spoke to me of possibility, of community, and of conversation. It was a very human piece. A class could meet in those chairs, discussing literature or philosophy. A church group might debate theological issues in this circle, or a village's elders might discuss matters about town. Or perhaps an intervention could be staged in the close confines of the space, or perhaps just a group of people sitting together in silent contemplation.

I gazed into the empty space amidst the chairs for a long time, only shaking out of my daze when a couple looked in over my shoulder, then walked away giggling. The next hallway I turned down ran along the western wall of the building, and shafts of glorious sunlight bathed sculptures made of twisted metal—works by John Chamberlain that resemble slices of car wrecks—then found myself face to face with my Dia:Beacon arch-nemesis.

One of my older sisters, a brilliant art history buff, had been trying to instill in me an appreciation for the works of Robert Ryman since the first time I had ever visited Dia:Beacon, on her recommendation. The Dia:Beacon Ryman exhibit showcases the abstract expressionist works he is best known for, works of white paint on white surface. Some of these are smooth, flat paintings while others have clumps and gnarls of paint here and there. My sister and I have stood before these paintings and she has explained to me the idea behind the work—the exploration and celebration of material and method, of brushstrokes and of the paint itself. My complaint to her has always been that it simply doesn't excite me aesthetically, and it's difficult for me to appreciate art on a purely conceptual level. I need my aesthetic senses to be stimulated. I walked into Ryman's section of the gallery with my arms crossed and a skeptical tilt to one eyebrow. I was calmer now than before.

Pondering *The Pure Awareness of the Absolute* seemed to bring the roiling surface of my inner psychedelic sea to a more placid place, gently sloshing where before it had been turgid and unpredictable. I stood before one Ryman painting, then another. I was in no rush, so I was completely lost in the moment with each painting for as long as I cared to be. I attempted to slough off my skepticism to give Ryman a chance.

But there was nothing doing. I walked out of Ryman's section and through a room housing works by On Kawara, a Japanese painter who paints the date in white block letters on a small black surface. These were all concept, so I found no aesthetic stimulation to be had there. I kept moving. Just outside the rooms housing Kawara's paintings was a door to a balcony outside.

I stepped out, looking over a tree-lined fence towards the railway lines just beyond the museum and past that, the Hudson River, speckled with ice and snow. I breathed in the crisp upstate air, my nostrils flooding with the fresh scent of the forest close by. A pair of birds wheeled overhead. I watched them for some time, simply breathing and feeling the coldness of the winter season. I felt hale and robust, and the breath visibly steaming out of my mouth seemed more alive than it had back in Brooklyn. I leaned on the railing of the balcony, looking out over the Hudson Valley. Waves of happiness lapped at me, and I felt that it would be easy to fall into them, to lose myself in ecstasy. It became a game of sorts—letting myself slip deeper into viscous pools of emotion, then calling myself back to my breath, to my center and the crisp air. Back inside, down a corridor, and around a corner I came upon Richard Serra's *Union of the Torus and the Sphere*. In truth, all my wanderings up until this point had been a sort of resistance against the gravity of that piece, and of the Serra works in the adjoining warehouse space. Set in a rectangular space just wide enough to barely contain it, *Union* evinced in me an immediate, visceral reaction of the sort I rarely experience with most modern works of art. A fiery tremor rumbled through my chest and abdomen as I stood beholding it, craning my neck, leaning one way and then the other.

The structure, wrought of two massive, conjoined plates of steel, absolutely dominates the space in which it has been placed. As the name implies, the two plates seem to have been cut from larger wholes, a torus and a sphere respectively, then fused together, forming some altogether novel amalgam of space and curve. There is an oceangoing feel about the piece, and with shafts of daylight slanting down from the windows set high in the walls on either side of it, my conception of it shifted quickly from boat to ark. On its spherical side, the structure leans towards one of the narrow walls of the room. As I walked by it I felt the enormous weight of it, the pressure of tons of steel, bearing down on me.

Paradoxically, I really enjoyed this experience of feeling as if at any moment I might be squished between steel and wall. I have a completely irrational fear that I discovered in my early teens when my father and I were on a trip and a business partner of his took us out fishing on a small boat he owned. Upon leaving the harbor, we had to navigate between a few humongous ships—cruise ships, tankers, military vessels—and I found myself paralyzed in utter fear. Since then I've had a handful of similar experiences of being surrounded by towering seagoing vessels and being absolutely petrified for no reason I can quite understand.

When I passed the narrowest point at which *Union* leaned towards its sphere-side wall, I let out a sigh of relief, but the kind you get when doing something risky that you know you'll do again. I circled around the other side of the mottled (the steel having oxidized into mesmerizing brown rust patterns) structure and paced down its other length. Here the torus leaned in on itself, bending away from the wall. From the torus side, *Union* seemed less like a boat and more like a wave. I stood at its centerpoint, with my back against the wall, and watched it tower above me, pulling away and then leaning back towards me at its uppermost point, as if I were standing at the foot of a huge, majestic rip-curl on the verge of crashing down.

I circled the structure again and again, entranced by the fact that I couldn't, from any angle, completely perceive it as a whole. I could only wrap my head around it in motion and even then, only barely. I stood with my back to the opposite wall for a time, at the point where the spherical half of the sculpture came closest, so that its long, slow curve nearly touched my nose. I breathed through the fear and anxiety that this triggered—latent emotions drawn into a heightened sensitivity by the phenethylamine in my system. When I finally walked away from *Union* and turned my back on it so that it was entirely out of my field of vision, I felt as if I had stepped into another scene in the film of my life.

The museum was going to close before long, and while there was much more I wanted to see—the mad scientist sculpture factory of Louise

Bourgeois on the top floor, Robert Smithson's poignant, raw works of dirt and glass—Serra had his hooks into me. I descended a flight of stairs that led down to the former train depot for the Nabisco box factory, a massive hangar-like space with windows placed high up in the walls all around. Entering the space, it feels as if you may have come upon some sort of secret government laboratory, where UFOs or their components have been stripped down for study. Four gigantic steel structures dominate the area, but there is enough space between and around them to allow one to get a broader perspective, unlike the tight squeeze of space surrounding *Union of the Torus and the Sphere*.

These are Serra's *Torqued Ellipses*. Each of the four is a variation on a common theme, and each of the four is fashioned from a two-inch thick, twenty-ton rolled steel plate. These four pieces, much like *Union*, aren't simply objects to be perceived with one's eyes, but sculptures that invite and need movement in order to engage with them.

One of the structures was a single hollow ring. I walked through the opening and stood inside of it, as light cascaded down over the high walls. An immediate sense of peace came over me, and I recalled standing outside on the balcony and looking out at the Hudson Valley, though now I was surrounded on all sides by a hard steel structure twice my height that threatened to envelope me. But the curve of the structure, and the sense of it bending slightly inwards towards me, wasn't in the least threatening.

Here was the same oceanic feeling I'd run up against with *Union of the Torus and the Sphere*, the sense of being suspended in a vast body of water, as if all the water in my body were suddenly becoming hyper-aware of itself and of its connection to the great seas that had pre-dated land and reptiles and mammals. I walked in a slow circle along the inside of the beautiful rust-colored sculpture, then out the thin open slit at one end. I toured the next two ellipses, noting how my body reacted to walking in tight spaces. One of the ellipses was actually a set of two: you entered on one end, then walked between its inner wall and the outer wall of a smaller ellipse set inside, until you got to the far end, where you entered the inner ellipse. I could hear voices of other museum visitors echoing in the space, and light and shadow seemed to jockey for my eyes' attention as I moved on slightly wobbly sea legs through the narrow corridor.

When I emerged at last into the center, it was a breath of fresh air. A group of elderly people stood to one end of the ellipse, talking in excited voices. It was all gibberish to me, and I thought that perhaps the drug's effects were still stronger than I'd surmised, since I felt that I was past the peak and easing into a gentle plateau. But as I listened more closely I realized they were speaking German and the harsh albeit beautiful sounds of the language were a bit much for me. My brain was having a hard time not seizing on to every sound they made, so I scurried out the way I'd come.

The third ellipse was structured similarly and I was relieved to find it empty. I sat down in the shadowed half of it, letting my eyes feast on the streaks and strange corrosions in the half of the steel ring still catching the rays of the slowly setting sun outside the hangar windows. A gentle sloshing sensation washed over me, not enough to dredge up any old nausea, just enough to make me feel as if I were in a canoe being lapped at gently by rolling waves. I heard the giggles of a small child and the rattle of footsteps resounding against the metal corridor through which I'd traveled to get here, and soon enough a small boy, perhaps four years old, emerged into the open space where I was seated, leaning back on my palms.

He'd been running but stopped in his tracks when he saw me and covered his face, peeking through his fingers at me, smiling but also looking unsure. We held eye contact for a moment and then his father emerged beside him. The little boy turned and hugged his father's leg, then ran back the way he came. The father looked at me and gave a friendly shrug, then walked back after his child. I left too after a few minutes, and made my way to *Torqued Ellipse IV*.

This ellipse was just one continuous plate of rolled steel, absolutely massive, curling in on itself like a cochlear canal. I walked through the spiral, the walls of the corridors curving inwards, so that it felt like the very space I was walking through was being molded and shaped by the ellipse. The corridor felt endless as I walked it, curling around itself again and again, so that I expected (as I always did, no matter how many times I visited) to emerge into a tight small space, far smaller than any of the centers of the other ellipses.

But when the spiral finally let out into an open atrium, it was more spacious than any of the prior ellipses. It was mind-bending. It didn't seem to make sense at all. It was like flowing out the mouth of a river or emerging into the world after traveling the length of the birth canal.

I was sure I'd walked right to the very small center of the spiral, but here I was in a space nearly the size of my apartment. I was suffused with a sense of safety, and again that oceanic feeling swept over me. I sat down on the ground, leaning back on my palms then down onto my back. After a time, I rolled onto my side, curling into a loose ball, feeling the cold concrete against me as I looked out at the sphere surrounding me and felt an almost overwhelming sense of peace. But, like on the balcony, the abyss of that bliss was something I only dabbled with, bringing myself back to my center by breathing.

I lay there for a time, and then heard footsteps slowly approaching. Thoughts of social codes of conduct and propriety surfaced in my mind, but I felt that I was in the right place, in the right position, even if I was, from an objective perspective, a drug-addled youth laying on the floor of a museum in the fetal position. I heard the sound of an Asian language, a deep male voice and a softer female voice, bouncing through the spiral corridor. I was on the floor in such a way that I faced the opening that let out into the central atrium of the ellipse.

A stunning young woman, perhaps in her mid-twenties, emerged first, and smiled when she saw me on the floor. A much older man, tottering in small steps and squinting through coke-bottle lenses, came after her, and seemed to avoid looking at me, turning and inspecting the wall of the space. I looked at the woman and we made eye contact as I propped myself up on one elbow and spoke, the sound of my voice strange to hear after hours of silent wandering.

"It's wonderful, isnt it?"

"Yes," she said, without hesitation. "When I come here, I feel like my subconscious has manifested itself into this incredible structure that surrounds me."

I couldn't have put it better myself.

Climbing back up the steps to the main floor of the museum, I felt renewed, baptized. I walked through the broad hallways, smiling as I watched my feet pad along the patterns in the wooden floor, suffused with a keen sense of serenity. All the anxiety had fled. A function of time, to be sure, as the phenethylamine was past its prime duration of action, but also the work of Serra and his *Torqued Ellipses*.

I took main hallways, avoiding walking through any of the galleries. I felt done with my trip to the museum, and ready to make it back to the station in time for the next train back to New York City. I passed works I had spent time with and many more—the gorgeous black and white photos of Bernd and Hilla Becher and the light art of Dan Flavin among them—that I hadn't had time to digest. Next time. I passed by the rooms housing Robert Ryman's works of white paint on white canvas and kept going.

Then I stopped. I backtracked, and ducked into Ryman's temple to texture, checking out the works once more. As I let my gaze soften and drift over the surface of each square and rectangle of paint, I saw, with a vision unfettered by the earlier, heavier effects of a psychedelic, the very precise and intricate track marks left behind by Ryman's process. There was no extra color quivering about, and no movement to the contours, edges, and soft lines. I thought back to the marks that oxidized each of Serra's works. Something had shifted. Ryman still bugged me, but what bugged me even more was that he wasn't bothering me as much as he had before. I felt drawn to the works, and compelled to give them their day in the sun. Much like my experience of circling *The Union of the Torus and the Sphere*, I was entranced by the tension between my inability to fully comprehend the work and my strong desire to penetrate to its essence.

The sun was on its downward arc as I returned along the path down to the train station. I had missed my train, and the next one wasn't due for fifteen minutes. The train station sat right by the Hudson and the wind whipping past was bitterly cold. A long dock jutted out from the shore into the river, frozen over about halfway out. Snow and ice coated the surface of the water and grew over the dock like winter fungus. I walked out on to the promontory (a signpost told me the long dock was in fact very astutely called Long Dock) and up to the point where it was frozen over, standing and looking out at the river and the seagulls wheeling over it, scanning the ice floes below for signs of life to pluck and eat.

As I waited for the train I looked out over the ice and snow that covered the river and saw how the process of freezing over, in the places where it had, was a gradual one. And that gradualness had led to the motion of the river being preserved in the way it froze. There weren't really any flat surfaces, just slow building ledges and curls, and what looked like the lines of waves and ripples etched into the freeze like a fossil in stone. I gazed at the surface of the water and thought about the process. I'd have to come back again sometime soon, and spend more time with the Rymans.

Arc Harp
Black Rock Desert
12mg 4-HO-MiPT

The electric gleam of LED lights and the sinuous eruption of flames along the horizon were shrouded in a thickening cloud of alkali dust as a massive windstorm descended on the Black Rock Desert in Nevada. The Burning Man Festival, that famous annual temporary city of some fifty-thousand inhabitants, had now been in full swing for the better part of a week. This was my first trip out to the playa, as the festival's annual revelers refer to the desolate desert landscape, the flat bottom of an ancient evaporated lake, where "Black Rock City" has been built and torn down almost every year since 1990. Veterans of this "temporary autonomous zone" had instilled in me a healthy respect for the power of the elements; I'd heard many stories about the dust storms that could paralyze the city in whiteout conditions, but my participation in the experiment had until now been marked by particularly glorious weather, day in and day out.

As my companion John and I rode our bikes out into the deep, open stretch of playa beyond the gridwork of the city proper, with twelve milligrams of 4-HO-MiPT bonding to the receptors in our brains, it was Friday. A full moon hung high above the desert and there was a mad, carnivalesque energy everywhere you looked. That was, of course, totally typical for any day in Black Rock City, but everything did seem particularly amped up on this, the penultimate night before the eponymous Man, the giant effigy at the center of the city, would be sent up in a riot of flames and fireworks.

Burning Man is renowned for teasing out the inner hedonist in its participants, and my camp companions, five close friends with whom I'd traveled from New York City, and I were no exceptions. Rather than "museum doses," we spent the week consuming what the late psychedelic visionary Terence McKenna had called "heroic" quantities of various substances, though it should be noted that the line between heroic and stupid is a fine and slippery one. I had taken Thursday off completely from indulging in any drugs, having been totally rattled by the events of that morning's sunrise. After being out all Wednesday night, I had been riding on the top of one of Burning Man's iconic mutant vehicles, a massive glittering spider, headed back to the city after witnessing what was truly one of the most spectacular, polychromatic sunrises of my entire life, a slow explosion of light that lifted reds and oranges and purples and pinks out of the dust all around us and shuffled them into the sky.

One of my closest friends, who I hadn't seen in two years before we reunited in the desert that week, was with me atop the wheeled spider, and on our way back to the city she suffered an accident that badly broke her ankle. Though it was no one's fault, I somehow felt responsible for her completely debilitating injury, which would not only ruin her week but probably have long-lasting repercussions for her active, athletic lifestyle. That previous night we had taken MDA, an MDMA analogue, and so the next day, coupled with the emotional drain of these feelings about my friend's pain, I was in a serious serotonin slump.

By the time the sun set on Friday night, I felt a bit better, and John wanted to get me out of my funk. My injured friend encouraged me to have fun as well. So, John and I decided to take a mild dose of 4-HO-MiPT. Twelve milligrams of that substance would be a comfortable museum dose even under normal conditions, but considering my substantial intake of various psychedelics throughout the week, whatever I took on Friday would have an uphill battle against tolerance. That was fine by me, as I was still feeling rattled enough that too heavy a trip could easily send me down a spiral of self-recrimination.

The word I often use to describe 4-HO-MiPT is "lush." It is a sensual drug with a pronounced body high and a euphoric drive to it that, at lower doses, doesn't feel pushy. At higher doses, however, it verges into deeply erotic territory and has provided me access to some of the most mind-blowing visuals I've ever experienced with psychedelics.

As soon as we hit the open desert, pedaling bikes illuminated by threads of LED wire in blue and pink and green, the wind began to seriously blow. We had no destination in mind—we were just out to enjoy ourselves and experience whatever strangeness we came across. We navigated from one cluster of humans to the next, checking out the foam-weapon battles in the Thunderdome, the massive effigy of Anubis set to burn later that night, a huge bird's nest made of plastic twist-ties, among other sights, all the while keeping up a friendly banter. John and I had been friends for some time, but in the lead-up to Burning Man and during the week itself, I had come to think of him as a brother. As the drug took subtle hold, I felt grounded in my body, home in my legs as they pedaled across the dusty expanse. I visualized a crystalline lattice of energy spreading through my body as I pedaled, tentacles of it reaching out across to John, meeting with his own, so that even while silent we communicated.

The full moon was so incredibly bright that it managed to shine fuzzily through the sheets of dust thickening all around us, even when, before long, visibility was otherwise almost nil. We parked our bikes for a moment while I adjusted the bandana covering the bottom half of my face, which had nearly come undone from a gust of wind, and wiped the dust that had accrued on my goggles. The fine alkali powder of the playa was swirling all around us, and when I held my hand as far out in front of me as I could, I couldn't see past the stump of my wrist. Suddenly continuing on seemed dangerous, both for us and for others—the danger of running into a piece of art or some clump of wandering dust-covered people was just too high.

John suggested we stand by our bikes for a while and just enjoy the dust storm whipping all around us. Gazing up at the luminescent moon I felt that latticework of energy rushing through my skin and my limbs, that feeling of the lushness of life flaring awake in every fiber of my being. And then we both became aware of a sound, close at hand, one we could hear even above the constant distant din of electronic bass beats that permeated the aural landscape morning and night at the festival. This was a gentler sound, a tinkling sequence of notes, of scales running up and down. The closer we listened, the closer they seemed to be, and we decided to walk towards them, making our way carefully through the dust clouds.

Suddenly, materializing out of the dust, we came upon a semicircular structure of about 300 degrees, which left an opening for people to walk in and out. The circle was solid up to about knee height, and then was completely open up to just above our heads, so that it was shaped much like an outdoor shower. Faint lines of red light quivered, disappeared and reappeared in the blowing dust, running like strings from the upper rim to the base. Seeing it through goggles, breathing beneath a dust mask, with the wind hissing all around us, I felt like an explorer on some desert planet stumbling upon a piece of ancient, alien technology.

A man stood outside the circle opposite from us, shirtless and goggled, and we watched him moving his hands in and out of the empty space in the circular structure, past the flimsy red threads of light. As he did so, we heard those sounds that had beckoned us. I stepped closer and watched the stranger, how each time he chopped his hands through the path of a laser, a note sounded out from speakers built into the structure.

Both John and I fanned out around the structure and began to pass our fingers through the beams of this laser harp, understanding quickly that each beam was tied to a particular note and that the notes climbed in scale from one end of the almost-circle to the other.

I always enjoy singing to myself, and in elementary school I had a brief, cacophonous fling with an alto saxophone, but while I have a deep appreciation for and visceral reaction to music of all types, I have never been particularly musical myself. I lived with a band of rock musicians for many years and would sit in on their jam sessions, perhaps contributing a solid tambourine rattle here and there, but always watching with awe at the seeming ease with which they expressed themselves through sound. They would often egg me on into joining them, but I would be crippled with anxiety and retreat in embarrassment to a safe, spectatorial distance.

As my hand passed through the laser harp's wispy, immaterial strings, none of that anxiety was present. My mouth slipped into a fishhook grin, and the sound emanating from the harp slipped into my eardrums and passed through my body so that I visualized, and felt, that latticework spreading through me all over again, brightening and quivering. I played one note at a time, jabbing my right hand in and out of the harp's invisible walls, and with no real plan in mind found myself constructing themes and melodies. When the thought occurred to me to throw my left hand into the mix, I did, and found to my surprise that I was, sonically at least, in that moment at least, ambidextrous. The more I played, the more I noticed that the speed with which I "plucked" the strings affected the sounds they made, their tempo and their duration.

I was completely consumed in my own relationship to the harp for some time, but soon I paused and listened to the sounds emanating from its speakers that weren't being caused by me. John and the stranger were playing their own tunes, walking along the length of the harp, playing separately but in concert, and as I began making music on the harp again myself, I became aware that though we weren't communicating verbally at all, nor even looking at one another (not that we could see much in the dusty gloaming), we were playing off of and with one another.

Some part of my mind was able to withdraw, pulling out the back of my head, detaching like a video camera, linked to me by that luminous network of energy I felt coursing through my being, and it watched us, like latter-day attendants on Godot, marooned out in the middle of the dusty desert void, speaking in laser tongues, three men shrouded in dust, writing a song that no one would ever hear.

Xu-Bing & Ai Wei Wei
St. John's Cathedral & Brooklyn Museum
10mg 4-AcO-DET

During the last week of December in 2013, I officiated an informal, somewhat impromptu wedding in Astor Court, the Ming Dynasty-style Chinese courtyard in the Metropolitan Museum of Art. After the brief, Philip K. Dick-quoting ceremony the couple, their parents, and I wandered the halls of the Asian Art wing. In addition to the permanent collection, there was a special exhibition on display dealing with the art of Chinese calligraphy through the ages. This was my first introduction to Xu Bing.

Along with an original piece of video art for the exhibition, there were retrospective photos of two famous works by Xu, *Book from the Sky* and *Square Word Calligraphy*. The former is a collection of invented calligraphic figures devoid of meaning, while the latter is a group of calligraphic figures made to resemble Chinese writing, though each figure is actually made up of English letters.

I have never had a knack for drawing or painting, but I have enjoyed playing with both mediums at times. I'd gone through a phase years earlier during which I would, usually under the influence of LSD, among other experiments dabble in a sort of automatic writing in which I would invent symbols and attempt to create alien languages. I really enjoyed the aesthetic qualities of the calligraphy on display at the Met, and I had a history of fascination with the idea of toying with language(s), so Xu Bing was on my radar, and when I heard he had installed a pair of sculptures in the immense space of St. John's Cathedral in Morningside Heights, my interest was piqued.

I had been conscious of Ai Wei Wei for some time already, though more as a public figure than for any particular work of art he had created. I had read many profiles about Ai, who, as just about everyone knows, had butted heads with the Communist Party in China for years and seemed to show, despite beatings, imprisonment, and trumped-up charges against him, no sign of slowing down. The Brooklyn Museum, a favorite local institution, had in recent years featured a string of major retrospectives of an incredible array of both American and foreign artists, and now it was one of four stops on Ai Wei Wei's touring exhibit "According to What?" The show would obviously never pop up in China. Ai can only really exhibit his art in the West.

It was late spring, and it had been an unusually long, cold, wet season, but as the sun climbed over New York City into a cloudless sky, temperatures spiked into the low eighties. It felt like the first true day of summer. After a light breakfast, during which I had been reading some of John Markoff's excellent book about the cross-pollination of the psychedelic counterculture and the computing scenes in 1960's and 1970's California, *What the Dormouse Said*, I packed a journal and canteen into a small backpack and ingested a capsule containing ten milligrams of 4-AcO-DET, a tryptamine described to me by close fellow travelers as being calm and mellow, which were attractive adjectives on such a marvelous day.

I felt a sense of liberation when I walked out into the dazzling bright day. A shimmering air of catharsis lay over the city as the welcome sheen of sweat condensed on people's skins. Winter, it seemed, was finally behind us. The streets of Brooklyn teemed with life. The shrieking excitement of small children at a street fair down the block felt contagious, but I managed to maintain adult composure and resisted the impulse to squeal out loud.

Forty-five minutes later I drifted out of a subway station on the Upper West Side, feeling only the faintest early glimmers of a trip, but even factoring in the bare naked sun beaming down, I did perceive an immediately noticeable sharpening of visual acuity—deeper saturation of color, starker detail, and amped-up brightness. The psychological aspects of the trip, however, seemed to hover at the periphery of my consciousness as I moved along the wide avenues of the now solidly gentrified neighborhoods of this part of upper Manhattan.

All my senses—even my perpetually impoverished sense of smell—were now ratcheting up a few notches. I heard each word of the multiple conversations of fellow pedestrians and sidewalk cafe patrons as I passed them by. Each human being I passed was a rich study in life's multitudinous expressions. Every detail of architecture was a world unto itself, reminding me of the famous episode of Aldous Huxley's losing himself in the wood grain of a chair on his first mescaline trip.

Yet this barrage of stimuli wasn't overwhelming in the slightest. In fact, with every step closer to my destination, I felt as if the processing power of my brain was increasing, taking in more data and unpacking it more deftly. I caught this train of thought and laughed at myself, since I knew how often I had tried to talk people down from the ledge of speaking of human personality and psychology in such mechanistic, technological terms, projecting our modern day advances on to our own organic framework.

I was reflecting on this when I turned the corner on 110th St. and beheld the Cathedral of St. John the Divine towering across the street, its Gothic facade evincing the visceral reaction that I have come to expect from the best religious architecture, which though erected in the names of dogmas with which I have many issues, almost always seem to be far more inspired—and inspiring—than the designs of even the most touted secular edifices. I was struck, too, once again, by the magnificence of my city, the infinity of awe it seemed to contain. I had lived here for thirty years before I could ever remember laying eyes on this massive structure.

I took a brief detour into the cathedral's garden courtyard to walk a few circles around a large bronze sculpture and fountain called Peace Fountain. The name seemed odd to me, in that while the sculpture did depict peaceful scenes of animals—one of St. John's particular niches—it all centered around the towering figure of the winged archangel Michael, who held a giant bronze sword, and at whose feet lay the decapitated, mangled corpse of Satan.

The sun was bearing down hard on Manhattan now, and I climbed the stairs into the welcome shade of the church. The last of the morning's worshippers were trickling out onto the street. It was shortly past noon, and having overslept and run late, I had just missed the Sunday choral services. I originally thought catching the services would have added another interesting layer to Xu Bing's installation, but in the end I was glad for my timing. The church, one of the largest in all Christendom, was now mostly empty.

The two open entrances to the church were smaller doorways on either side of the massive, twenty-foot tall bronze doors looming over the set of steps leading down to Amsterdam Avenue. I ducked in one of these and passed a few well-heeled supplicants on their way out as I walked into the incredibly tall and even longer nave, which seemed to stretch on endlessly into the distance. The ceilings, well over a hundred feet above my head, were ringed by numerous stained glass windows set high into the walls.

I felt the space keenly. Each breath I took felt deeper here. And staring me in the face as I walked into the nave were Xu Bing's two phoenixes. These weren't creatures from a myth or a fantasy novel so much as they were artifacts from a dystopian future. They had a distinctly steampunkish feel. Both birds had been hung in a way that suggested motion, suspended by cables from massive girders and trusses built into the

Gothic nave. I could imagine them in motion, slithering through the air.

Each was constructed from a variety of material harvested from construction sites in urban China, both building materials and tools as well as remnants from the daily lives of migrant laborers, whose villages Xu Bing had seen while touring the construction site of Beijing's World Financial Center, where he had been commissioned to make an installation. Horrified by the conditions that he had seen, he chose to construct two giant phoenixes, one of the most potent creatures of Chinese myth, as symbols of rebirth and of dreams. His backers ended up demanding that he coat the phoenixes' rusty, junk-crafted bodies with crystals and gems if they were to be housed in the World Financial Center. He declined, and the rejected birds have been touring the West since.

I scanned the bodies of each bird as I walked beneath them, feeling dwarfed, and they in turn appearing tiny, for all their hugeness, in this cavernous environment. Tubes, shovels, jackhammers, strips of metal, all wove together to form these bodies. Their torsos were made out of iron sheets of metal pleated into scales and shredded into strips that curled into thin spiral threads that conveyed an impression of wind currents swirling around their bodies. Red and white and blue ribbons stretched back, swaying like tails, looking like the shed skin of a paper dragon in the Chinese New Year Parade.

Now and then I spotted small propellers embedded in the massive frames, as well as rows of empty propane tanks. I could imagine the birds actually flying. Small bluish LED lights glowed like trim all along the contours of the two birds, but not at all too brightly, which only lent itself further to the dystopian desert feel of the pieces. I thought of a science fiction book I had read recently, *Roadside Picnic*, in which humans dig up alien technology they don't know how to use. I imagined a story in which these birds had been discovered in an archaeological dig, remnants of a time before human ascendancy, creations of some ancient mechanical phoenix culture, and all our scientists could do was set the lights in them glowing, and hang them for all to see.

Behind the phoenixes' heads—with chains dangling like whispers from mouths built out of propane tanks, suggesting fiery breath—were glass-plated segments around their shoulders that looked like the cockpits of ancient flying machines. I passed under the last tail feather of the second phoenix and into the central crossing of the church. Ahead of me was the pulpit with all its candles and icons and a bevy of Christian imagery. I walked halfway towards it, then turned around.

The phoenixes looked even more alive from behind, fleeing the pulpit, as if they'd just been loosed from the belfry and were about to knock open the massive bronze doors and wreak havoc upon Manhattan in a montage of destruction fit for a blockbuster film. I knew they were supposed to be symbols of triumph and hope, not of destruction, but my science fiction brain was running away with the material provided. I liked these phoenixes. I thought they were very cool, and planned on coming back before they were taken down at the end of the year.

The 2 and 3 trains weren't far, and it took me about forty-five minutes to get to the Brooklyn Museum. The subway, though completely and utterly packed with reveling travelers on this gorgeous Sunday, was surprisingly bearable. Even in my heightened state, even when at the Times Square Station a gaggle of tourists pressed in about me on all sides, one gigantic family trip, I was able to retain my equanimity, though I was envisioning a sort of intellectual exoskeleton sprouting from my mind, digital tentacles reaching out and gathering information speedily and efficiently—mechanistic metaphors again.

I thought back to the book I had been reading at breakfast, *What the Dormouse Said*, and realized that this drug experience aligned quite nicely with the vision of one of the story's central protagonists, Douglas Engelbart, a pioneer of human-computer interaction who viewed computers as being useful not as replacements for human intelligence but as tools for augmenting human consciousness, creativity, and potential. "Augmentation" fit the bill precisely for this tryptamine.

As I walked back out into the Brooklyn air, which always seems fresher and lighter than its Manhattan counterpart, I was feeling quite pleased with the completely unobtrusive nature of this psychedelic experience, the way it positively enhanced at the periphery without at all clouding the center.

The Ai Wei Wei exhibit at the Brooklyn Museum took over two whole floors of the museum. I squeezed into a crowded elevator, all of whose occupants were headed to the fifth and top floor, where the exhibit started. It was a busy Sunday afternoon for museum-going. This turned the whole Ai Wei Wei exhibit into a bit of a maze, since in a fashion I find typical of the curation at the Brooklyn Museum, the curators had packed as much art as possible into each room of the exhibit. Really compounding this, though, was a gigantic tour group being led by a tour guide with a particularly piercing, nasal tone of voice and what struck me as a sort of kindergarten-level tenor to her comments.

All around me in the first room were incredibly cool-looking pieces of woodwork and a series of beautiful black and white photographs from a period in the 1980s and 1990s when Ai lived in New York City during the AIDS epidemic, an experience that would inform his activism about AIDS in China, a topic the government is eager to sweep under the rug. I squirmed past the shuffling tour group and squeezed into a side room to watch a long depressing video about a Chinese woman who had contracted AIDS and was pressured by the local government to stay home and stay quiet. It was a powerful portrait, but unfortunately just when I felt myself really getting lost in it, the tour group pressed in around me.

I fled down to the fourth floor, close to giving up on the exhibit altogether and deciding to come back another day. The 4-AcO-DET was more noticeable now, approximately three hours in, than it had been all day. I started feeling unpleasant bodily sensations. Like so many of us, I typically carry a lot of stress in my shoulders, and the muscles that lead up to my neck from them are often tough as gnarled ropes. Now it felt as though my trapezius muscles were both tightening and pulling upwards.

After some stretching I felt a bit more relaxed, and the fourth floor, the bottom floor of the exhibit, was mercifully quieter. Only a few fellow museum-goers were about. From the stairs I turned left into a room where a giant snake coiled along the ceiling. It reminded me of the phoenix a bit, in that it was a creature made of found objects. Here, though, the objects weren't construction materials but backpacks.

An info card told me that the backpacks were the same type popular with children in Sichuan province, where a gigantic earthquake had, in 2008, killed thousands of people, many of them schoolchildren. The Chinese government released no official figures related to the deaths, nor did they accept any culpability, though thousands of children died when shoddily-built official government schools collapsed on them. Incensed by this, Ai launched what he called a citizens' investigation into the tragedy, from which this and other artworks were also born.

I looked back up at the snake, and it was impossible not to imagine the dead, mangled bodies of innocent children strapped to each of them. There was something different at play here than Xu Bing's attempt to sculpt beautiful creatures out of ramshackle construction materials. Those phoenixes had been beautiful, but this snake, while certainly colorful, had an ugly, almost venomous tone to it. I could feel the anger coiled in it, and having to look up at it, having it draw and demand my attention, was powerful.

The snake was just a warm-up, though. In the next room was a massive, low sculpture titled *Straight*, made of row upon row upon row of rusted, dirty rebar, poles of reinforced steel used in concert with concrete when building. The rusty bars, one hundred and fifty tons of them, form a landscape that has a rift running through it, suggestive of the tectonic plates that shifted to cause the earthquake. Most striking, though, is that the bars themselves do in fact come from the Sichuan earthquake. Ai and his team went through the laborious process of straightening each bar, which had been mangled in the destruction, back into its original straight form, as if nothing had ever happened, which is how he felt the government was trying to deal with the entire event, to act as if everything was fine and no one had died.

I walked the length of the sculpture slowly, my eyes picking out every little detail of each bar, every fleck of rust, every difference in level as the piles grew higher or smaller, that visual acuity still running full force, my perceptual exoskeleton still interfacing with my surroundings. On a wall to my right were the names of those who had died in the earthquake. Though these names were written in Chinese, and I could not understand them, the same names were being recited over a speaker in the room, each by a relative of the deceased. And though I could not understand those names either, the fact that they were being spoken by a loved one gave them immense power.

Straight, like the snake on the ceiling, was an ugly thing. I felt my own anger and sadness at an event that, until now, I had felt typically distant from as a relatively comfortable Western urbanite whose only connection to the earthquake in 2008 was through the media, at which time I felt an upwelling of compassion. But that upwelling drifted off into the ether, as it does with any disaster, simply as a function of the passage of time and the drifting of that news story deeper into the back pages.

A few days later I had the opportunity to meet with an art history scholar who is of Chinese descent and is familiar with the works of both Xu Bing and Ai Wei Wei. I hadn't known before my psychedelic day of contemporary Chinese Art that the two artists had formerly been friends but had experienced, especially recently, a deepening rift between them. Ai feels betrayed by Xu Bing, who did not speak out in his defense as the Chinese authorities increasingly cracked down on him. Xu, who lived in New York City at the same time as Ai, has returned to China and risen to become the second in command of the prestigious, and official, Central Academy of Fine Arts, while Ai has remained a thorn in the side of the authorities.

Looking back now on the two installations, they make much sense in this context, and ultimately, Ai's work hit me much harder than Xu's. Is it a competition? Not exactly, but perhaps. After all, though I knew that Xu's phoenixes were meant as critical commentary of working conditions, I see now how that criticism required compromise due to his position. And in the end, I walked away from his phoenixes with less of a sense of their criticism than a sense of their coolness. My reaction to Ai's work, however, was visceral, even if on an aesthetic level it wasn't as interesting.

As I walked home from the Brooklyn Museum that afternoon, it was only four PM, and I felt just slightly above baseline when I returned home to my apartment. A four-hour trip is an ideal length when one doesn't want to sign away an entire day, and it had been so mellow and unobtrusive that I really felt very positively about the experience, but there's always a price to pay, and once I was in my apartment I became keenly aware of the tightness in my trapezius muscles once more. I guess that was the toll exacted for the temporary activation of this perceptual augmentation system.

I sat down on my couch after stretching. I felt sober but energized. Tryptamines often seem to have a stimulating quality that lasts long after their psychedelic effect has run its course, and I decided to harness that energy. I picked up my trustiest augmentation device—my bicycle—and set out for the park, deciding to spend the rest of the afternoon lavishing the same sort of attention on my body that I had given to my mind.

Egon Schiele: Portraits
Neue Galerie
13mg 4-HO-MET

A glorious spring day dawned in New York City. All over town people fled from the claustrophobic confines of their apartments out into the streets and parks, desperate for open spaces after a punishing, endless winter. I was in fantastic spirits. Months of soul-searching had reached their climax in the past week. I had given notice to my work, where I had been employed for some nine years. I had broken the news to my family as well—that after spending my entire life here, I would be leaving the city and getting some wandering under my belt, after which I'd settle down in a new metropolis some thousands of miles away.

I felt free, and with the sunshine pouring in through my windows, I decided a trip was in order. It had been nearly a year since I'd last delved into my pharmacopeia. In that time I had sat in a handful of ayahuasca ceremonies, but those were as much intentional ordeals as they were adventures. As I picked my poison for this day's trip, a warm tryptamine made the most sense. I felt completely lighthearted. This would be a reward of sorts for having worked through layers of fear and anxiety to commit to following a dream.

A glittering bindle made from a friend's stash of arts and crafts supplies held a sample she'd bequeathed to me—thirteen milligrams of 4-HO-MET. I'd been saving it for a special occasion. A favorite molecule of many fellow psychonauts, it was known for being a crowd-pleaser as far as visuals were concerned, and I couldn't recall hearing a negative thing about it. I swallowed the psilocin analog and headed out.

The sun was warm but the air was crisp—that perfect transitional weather that marks the release of winter's icy grip. My Brooklyn neighborhood thrummed with life, nothing like the grey desolation of just a week earlier. On the subway platform awaiting the C train, I was surprised to feel the onset of the drug curling its way into my awareness only fifteen minutes in. It started in my gut and was already rising most insistently. I felt immediately that this drug wouldn't wash over me in waves; this ride was going to be one long arc.

My destination was an Egon Schiele exhibit at the Neue Galerie on Manhattan's Upper East Side, a museum devoted to 20th Century German and Austrian art that opened in 2001 but that I had never visited. It was a long way off from my apartment, and the journey to get there would take me right through the heart of Manhattan. I changed trains at the newly redesigned/rebuilt post-9/11 subway complex at Fulton Center, all its metallic surfaces and alien-spaceship-like designs glistening with newness.

By the time the 5 train arrived I was fully in the thrall of a spiraling pulse of energy. It originated in my gut, emanated outwards through my chest cavity, and brushed the bottoms of my feet and the dome of my skull before it radiated out into the world around me. I felt as if I might outgrow my body, as if my mind, the drug, my body, the world around me, were having difficulty getting into sync. It was a blessing when, on the extremely crowded subway car, someone seated right beside where I was standing got up to exit and I was able to slip down into the seat, no longer needing to pad back and forth from one foot to the other in an attempt to displace the energy building up in me. I melted into the seat instead.

I was in the middle of the car and swiveled my head back and forth to take in the whole panorama, the multitude of faces and colors and emotions, the babbling brook of language spilling dissonantly into the space of the car. The further into Manhattan we pushed the more and more people crowded in. Each added ingredient threatened to tip the precarious balance in my mind, the precarious hold I had on being able to stomach so much going on at once.

I was at once enthralled and repulsed by all the human faces surrounding me. The smiles and lively eyes and nuances of emotions fascinated me, but I felt oppressed by the odors and mannerisms and all the little cues of insanity that crop up whenever millions of people are thrown together. As we passed below the densest loci of commerce and tourism in Manhattan—Herald Square, Times Square—the train filled to capacity and I felt as if I might explode. Sealed in this rumbling can with so many other humans, my senses were cranked to eleven. I needed escape.

By the time the train arrived at 86th Street I had calmed myself through some deep breathing with eyes closed. I squirmed through sweaty bodies to get out of the car and climbed the long stairwell up to the street. The city seemed to birth itself into existence around me. I felt as though I was expanding to fill the space all around me, the city's grid. As I turned corners the metropolis continued to build itself, bathed in dazzling sunlight.

Motion seemed to be the key. When I had to stop at a traffic light, the energy spiral building up inside of me became nearly unbearable, but once able to cross I could channel the pulse into my steps, and I felt supremely embodied, which isn't often the case for me. I tend to live in my head, and I have to push myself to remember to exercise and eat healthily. This was a pleasant feeling, to be fully in my body, to feel every muscle and bone move as I walked.

The Neue Galerie was across the street, occupying a 100-year old Beaux-Arts mansion at the corner of 5th Avenue. A huge line snaked out from the door. I hadn't counted on that, but I was glad for the excuse to wait a bit before going in. Just across Fifth Avenue, spacious and open with plenty of space to wander, was Central Park.

I entered the Park by the Jacqueline Kennedy Onassis Reservoir, not a typical haunt of mine when I made my way up here. I found myself drawn to it this time, especially to the natural curve it offered, so I climbed up to the pathway encircling it and leaned up against the railing, looking out over the liquid field. The wind drummed fantastic wave patterns into the water, while the sky above was almost completely cloudless. An airplane cut silently overhead and I found myself dazed, watching its progress, suppressing for a moment the keening anxious push to keep moving that was swelling inside me.

And then, a noxious thought came to me. All urban trippers willingly put themselves in a situation where a bit of paranoia is likely to surface: one is doing something illegal, and one feels so altered that the fear of revealing oneself by being conspicuously strange in behavior is inevitable. Hence the "museum dose"—just enough, but not too much. But the thought came: I am a shaggy-haired, somewhat poorly shaven guy with a big backpack, standing at the Central Park Reservoir, watching a plane overhead. A cascade of images and sensations washed over me—the surveillance state, September 11th, the illegality of my pharmacopeia, the fact that this city was more closely watched than ever. I understood what a black hole this line of thought could be, but a great sadness welled up in me, sadness that I was having these thoughts at all, that this activity was illegal, that my city was so wounded that it had become so heavily monitored, and that I was standing here on a beautiful day stuck in this thought loop.

Movement. I knew movement would help. I stepped away from the railing and walked along the perimeter of the reservoir. Most of the trees were still leafless, though they seemed to buzz with the promise of plumage. All around me people were walking, bicycling and running. The parade of characters was stunning. One gigantic beast of a man loped up on to the trail, heaving his immensely muscled body along one slow running step at a time. In one hand he held a humongous sledgehammer that he would repeatedly toss in the air in front of him, and after it flipped once, catch in his other hand and repeat, a god descended from Olympus jogging among the mortals.

Families were out, as were other solitary walkers, joggers, birdwatchers, old women, and shabby vagrants sprawled out across park benches with sun-drenched grins on their faces. I walked around the reservoir and around once more, circling it three or four times before I finished; I lost count. I was dazzled. The staggering possibilities of existence were laid out before me, and the setting for all these myriad incarnations was my city. Sometimes I would pause, touching a hand to the railing that circled the body of water, and gaze out at the glistening skyscrapers across the way, feeling my heart aching in my chest with a longing for something I had not even left yet.

The spiritual work of the past months, the dark winter, had for me been centered on building trust in myself. Walking along the reservoir, smiling at laughing children running past me, I felt faith in myself, in my decision. It was time to go, but that didn't stop the whole walk from being tinged with a potent melancholy. This city was the only home I'd ever known.

I checked the time and was shocked to see that it was four-thirty, but when I took stock of the trip and sensed that things had calmed a bit, it made sense that so much time had passed. The museum would close at six, so I finished my last loop around the reservoir and walked back toward it. When I turned the corner at 86th St., I walked right into a sharply dressed old man who was at the end of the line of people waiting for the museum. The line! I had to laugh. This was part of New York, too, after all: eternally waiting to be admitted. I apologized to the gentleman and waited, patiently.

I was four hours into the journey now and expected to be past the plateau as I entered the museum, but stepping into closed quarters only seemed to amplify the trip significantly. Speaking was difficult, even if all I needed to muster for entry was "one, please" and "no, thank you" when offered an audio tour.

I was coming into this exhibit with very little knowledge of Schiele aside from a sketch of his biographical details—born in the last decade of the 19th Century, he was an immensely prolific young talent who blossomed under the mentorship of Gustav Klimt. Schiele died very young, at 28, but left behind a huge body of work. The exhibit came on my radar via word-of-mouth, and I had purposely avoided studying up on it beforehand.

The interior of the Neue Galerie was sleek and starkly modern, contrasting with the classical design of the building it lived in but not conflicting at all, a masterful piece of German design. A set of marble stairs climbed up to the third floor of the gallery, where the Schiele exhibit lived. Just before I reached the third floor, the staircase curved past a four-foot-tall black and white image of Schiele himself. A wave of hair swept back from a forehead wrinkled with curiosity, and eyebrows played flirtatiously with the camera pointed at his intelligent face. I could tell that he and I were going to get along famously.

The stairwell opened up onto a corridor with four rooms to choose from, and I ducked into the closest one to me. Eddies of light were rippling along the white walls and washing over the very many portraits hung all around the room. The sheer volume of artworks was dizzying. Complicating matters was that I couldn't focus on any one portrait at all. Here in the confines of the gallery I was aware, in a way that the open space of Central Park never hinted at, of the intense activity in my eyes. I would attempt to train my vision on one portrait at a time (all in this room were smaller, with frames layering the walls nearly top to bottom), but my eyes simply would not sit still. The light in the room was amplified, washing out the details of each portrait as I tried to focus on them. I was annoyed at the drug: it was insinuating itself between me and the art in a way that only obfuscated, rather than enhanced.

I padded from one portrait to the other, feeling agitated, the spiraling energy inside me still alive if a bit more relaxed. This room was too much, so I stepped out into the corridor running through the exhibit, in search of another place to invest my energy. I was drawn immediately to a very dark room just across the hall. It was a small, even claustrophobic space, and I stilled myself by reading, very slowly, training my focus, the text explainer on the wall. In the spring of 1912, at the age of 22, Schiele was imprisoned on multiple charges (including abduction and rape) for his sexual involvement with a girl below the age of consent in a quiet village outside the capital Vienna.

This darkened room collected the works Schiele had produced during this formative period in his career. At his trial, the judge burned one of the explicitly pornographic drawings seized from Schiele's apartment. The works in this room reflected his anger and anguish, but more than any of the pieces that depicted his life in his prison cell, I was drawn to a rainbow spiral of geometric blocks of color that circled a stark point of blackness at its core. I was totally entranced by this simple, childlike drawing. There was nothing particularly masterful about it, but its poignancy cut right to my core. I felt reflected in it. I looked to the title and smiled: *My Life's Wandering Path Carries Me Over Abysses.*

I meditated for some time on that black space and the colors that converged around it. People came and went, and I lost all track of time. When I finally pulled myself away, an oceanic tranquility had washed over me. The spiraling was still there, but much calmer, like a snake charmed into somnolence. I left the darkened room, passing a cast of Schiele's death mask, and turned left into the largest room of the exhibit.

Directly across from me as I entered hung the flagship image of the exhibit, a life-size portrait of Schiele's wife Adele wearing a rainbow-striped skirt with a matching button-down rainbow top over a white blouse, a shy smile playing on her lips beneath bright eyes. I turned away from it, with my own shy smile, and made my way along the left hand wall of the room. Here was a collection of Schiele's erotic works that had so scandalized his fellow citizens. They were considered extremely lewd for Schiele's time, but remarkably, in many ways they were even lewd for our current much cruder, less inhibited era.

Red was the most fascinating color in these drawings, which portrayed women alone or together in highly sexualized poses, sometimes with Schiele interposed as well. Some drawings simply showed Schiele masturbating, squinting over his shoulder at the "camera." As I allowed my eyes to linger and surf across each portrait, it slowly dawned on me just how grotesque they were, but that realization was only secondary to my thrill at their beauty. I found the drawings beautiful, and the people in them beautiful, but the more I looked at them the more I also realized how raw and ugly and deformed they were.

Midway through the central wall of this room stood Schiele's wife, Adele, in the painting titled *Portrait of the Artist's Wife, Standing*. She took my breath away, broke my heart with the sweetness with which he'd painted her. Her seeming delicacy and innocence were a stark contrast to the prostitutes and unfettered sexuality displayed in Schiele's erotic work. She stood in her rainbow-striped clothing, her fingers curled inward towards her palm as if unsure of what to do with them. A gentle blush played along her cheeks, bursting from ghostly pale-skin but matching the auburn of her coiffed hair. Between blushing cheeks and swirls of hair sat two eyes that popped out towards me, as if her whole being was barely contained in this mawkish frame.

I sat on a cushion in the middle of the room, directly across from Adele, and lost myself in her, or maybe not in her, but in Schiele's adoration of her. There was a theme running through all of Schiele's portraits, the attempt to capture a person's essence beyond the limitations of the body. And Adele's essence was perfection. I noted that hers was possibly the only portrait in the collection that possessed anything remotely approaching symmetry, so commonly considered a key indicator of beauty.

I couldn't tear my eyes from her hands. They looked so hard-worked, and in the way that red blood blushed in the vessels running through her knuckles

I could sense how Schiele must have loved those hands, those fingers. How he must have kissed them, held them in his own, worshipped them.

All track of time fled. I had to pull myself away.

Moving on to the other half of the room, I journeyed through Schiele's self-portraits. Some dated to his very early adolescence. They were much simpler than his later drawings, but still showed that particular knack for evoking spirit with nothing more than lines. As they progressed through time, though, you could actually see a human being coming to a deeper and deeper understanding of himself, not that the self-portraits increasingly hewed to some sort of higher ideal or true representation, but rather that they embraced the multitudinous nature of consciousness. Not one Schiele, but many Schieles. The faces of Schiele—sometimes playful and coy, at other times glowering and resentful, or haughty and proud, as in *Self-Portrait with Peacock Waistcoat*. Still others were absolutely haunting and skeletal, paintings in which Schiele looked like the survivor of a prison camp, his skin clinging to the rigid outline of bone. But in these, his spirit still shone, determined, out of his eyes and mouth.

As I lingered on some of the darker self-portraits, I meditated on common trends in the current glut of so-called psychedelic or visionary art. So often there was a tendency among these artists to represent people as luminous light-beings, as if the raw reality of our gross physical existence were nothing more than illusion. Schiele, I thought, had the deeper understanding: bodies were in fact a vital part of the equation, of the reality of our existence, but no matter how raw or ugly they might be, the indomitable spirit can still flare brightly from within.

I'm not normally drawn to portraiture; my taste in art is often more abstract. But all these portraits, and especially the self-portraits, had their hooks in me. There was a truth to them that seemed unassailable. The lines of the faces—so exact yet so free, so simple yet so nuanced—evoked rich layers of personality. Those faces, however, led to bodies, and the bodies were without fail rough, skeletal, or sickly, seeming to sort of dangle away from the heads of their wearers as mere vessels. And red was the lifeblood in these vessels, burgeoning at knuckles and cheeks and joints and labia, all the parts of the body that most feel the hard flush of life.

I'd missed one room, which I headed to next; this featured large portraits Schiele had done of colleagues and mentors. I gravitated to one portrait in particular, *Portrait of Karl Zakovsek*, depicting one of Schiele's fellow painters. I'd gotten the fancy from Schiele's self-portraits that, in all his playfulness and perceptiveness, he was a character whose company I would have really enjoyed had I been alive at the same time as him. In this portrait, Karl Zakovsek reclined against an unseen wall, his right hand held against his cheek and jaw, his sleepy face resting and regarding me, or Schiele, with a warm openness. He wore a simple suit jacket and button-down shirt, and his hair reminded me of my own, puffing up at the top as it did. He was alarmingly thin, with bone-like fingers, and we had the same scruffy simple beard and hint of a mustache. The longer I looked at Karl Zakovsek, the more I felt like I was staring into a mirror. I'd seen that Schiele had an intensely perceptive eye for the various forms of humanity, and now I felt I was seeing that, archetypally at least, perhaps I had existed at the same time as him, or at least my doppelganger had.

Sometimes a work of art tells you when it's time to leave, and I felt that Karl was letting me know it was time to go. My cup overflowed. I started for the exit, but as I passed through the hallway I could see Adele in her rainbow dress in the distance. I walked down the hall and went to stand in front of her a little longer. It struck me, then, that she represented a union. On my left were the works of Schiele's eros, and on the right those of his id, and here stood Adele, bringing the two sides of one man into union. It was impossible not to romanticize the artist and his relationship to his wife. They died shortly after marriage, together, as the Spanish Flu ravaged Vienna in the very closing days of World War I. Perhaps if they hadn't died (and what an irony, for Schiele to die in such a frail physical way), they would have divorced; perhaps Schiele's star would have waned, but it didn't matter, because here stood Adele, a testament.

I stood bathed in her rainbow radiance as a young girl approached the painting. She looked nerdy and sickly, with a chalky pallor to her skin, thick-lensed glasses on her eyes. She was perhaps fifteen or sixteen, and looked shyly at the portrait of Adele, a small smile playing at her lips. She chewed the bottom one. It was amazing, really; they too were doppelgangers. And most striking or perhaps ridiculous of all, she was wearing a floppy jester's cap in six vibrant colors of the rainbow that matched the dress in the painting. This girl seemed just the type of weirdo that Schiele might have painted. I felt like this was her moment now with Adele, and so I turned, and left the museum for the bright and busy Manhattan streets.

Evening was settling down upon the city. The crispness that had hung in the air all day now asserted itself. I took some deep breaths and felt at peace. Was it just the timeline of the drug, or was it the communion I had just experienced, connecting across space and time with the vision of an artist whose appreciation, and perhaps revulsion at the many faces of humanity that swam all around him, echoed my own feelings?

Once home, I settled down on a cushion on the floor, resting in my breath. The swirl of spring sounds outside my window oscillated between cacophony and symphony. I looked around my apartment, at the way my identity was reflected in the colors and objects that littered my tables and decorated my walls. Soon it would all be dismantled And when it came together again, how would it be different? How would I be different? Just who was I, and how much of me was centered here?

A week later, I came home to a postcard in the mail. It was a 4x6 reprint of the *Portrait of Karl Zakovsek*, with his sleepy eyes and skeletal hands. Who sent this? I turned it over and saw the familiar curlicues of an old lover's tight handwriting. It was she who had most encouraged me to go to the Schiele exhibit. The card was postmarked from a few days before I'd finally done so.

D-

This guy so reminds me of you. Pensive. A little sad. A little attitude. A new haircut. About to smile.

-M

Daniel Tumbleweed is a native New Yorker. A mild-mannered bookkeeper by day, he enjoys DIY art spaces and world-class galleries equally by night. His greatest psychedelic regret is missing an opportunity to trip at the Brooklyn Museum's Fred Tomaselli retrospective in 2010.

J.P. Harpignies is the author of: *Double Helix Hubris* (1997), *Political Ecosystems* (2004), *Delusions of Normality* (2009), and *Animal Encounters* (2014); co-author of *The Magic Carpet Ride* (2011); editor of the collection, *Visionary Plant Consciousness* (2007); and associate editor of *Ecological Medicine* (2004) and *Nature's Operating Instructions* (2004).

www.ingramcontent.com/pod-product-compliance
Ingram Content Group UK Ltd.
Pitfield, Milton Keynes, MK11 3LW, UK
UKHW041639190726
13854UKWH00006B/2598

9 780692 446447